MAGIC SEEDS FOR SUCCESS

Reflections for Personal Growth

MAGIC SEEDS FOR SUCCESS

Reflections for Personal Growth

Napoleon Hill
&
Judith Williamson

Published by
PRABHAT PRAKASHAN PVT. LTD.
4/19 Asaf Ali Road,
New Delhi-110 002 (INDIA)
e-mail: prabhatbooks@gmail.com

Published in India by arrangement with
The Napoleon Hill Foundation
PO Box 1277, Wise, Virginia 24293, USA

ISBN 978-93-5186-778-4
MAGIC SEEDS FOR SUCCESS
by Napoleon Hill & Judith Williamson

Edition
2025

Price
₹ 250.00 (Rupees Two Hundred Fifty only)

Printed at
Royal Offset, Delhi

Introduction

Judith Williamson is the ideal author to take Napoleon Hill's writings and create reflections for her readers. When I first read the manuscript that you now have in your hands, I felt like I was back in the classroom and the course was Dr. Hill's Science of Success.

It has been said that when the student is ready, the teacher will appear. Both you and I know that the answers we seek are within each of us, but it often takes someone else to show us the direction in which to proceed. If you are a student of life and desire to be more successful, then by all means let Dr. Hill and Judith Williamson be your teachers.

As a personal word of advice, expect to be a better person when you have read *Napoleon Hill's Magic Seeds for Success,* studied the material, and have taken action on the book's principles.

It is not the accumulation of what you read that matters, but what you use. It only takes a few weeks of repeating the same act until it becomes a habit–either a good habit or a bad one. I know you have probably heard the saying, "we first make our habits and then our habits make us."

Do not measure the value of a book by the complexity of the advice it gives. W. Clement Stone, Dr. Hill's most famous student and business partner states: "You cannot write your own prescription for a pair of glasses, but you can write your own prescription for correcting your mental vision."

His pertinent advice simply directs you to write your own mental vision for your life in a few sentences. Yet it is interesting to note in a novel the author determines the ending, while in a self-help book, the reader determines the ending.

Just as millions of other Napoleon Hill readers have done for nearly one hundred years, the message you are to receive, if you are ready to receive it, is that there is a roadmap to success. You can attain the success in life most people only dream of attaining. But, first you must follow in the footsteps of those who have achieved their goals.

Enjoy the journey.

Don Green, Executive Director
The Napoleon Hill Foundation

Magic Seed 1

Your capacity to believe is your greatest potential asset.

–NAPOLEON HILL

Dear Readers:

Do you rub a magic lamp, carry a rabbit's foot, wish upon a star, pray for a windfall, read your horoscope, consult the Tarot, gaze into a crystal ball, or consult psychics? Well, if you do, you are looking without for your success instead of looking where most people never think to look–within! True magic is within us not outside of us.

W. Clement Stone, Dr. Hill's student, friend and partner states: "Awaken the sleeping giants within you! They are more powerful than the Genii of Aladdin's lamp. Their power is staggering. The Genii are fictional. Your sleeping giants are real."

The sleeping giant slumbers inside you and you are the only one who can wake this Genie up. This sleeping giant is an aspect of yourself that perhaps you have not attempted to awaken before because you never knew that he was slumbering right inside your mental threshold. Isn't it time you sounded the alarm clock?

Once you realize that no one or nothing can awaken the giant within you except yourself, you begin to search for a "wake up call" in a more precise and disciplined manner. I have often said that Thought + Action = Success. This is as good a formula as any for helping us figure out that the very "magic" we are seeking is placed inside us by Infinite Intelligence for each of us to discover in due time.

There are tools in our toolkit that can help us discern

where we are going and what we are here for, but we must begin by knowing that if our only tool is a hammer, much appears as if it needs hammering. If you have restricted yourself to one tool for uncovering your success, why not try a few new ones? Learn how your subconscious mind works. Add autosuggestions, journaling, vision boards, affirmations, reading, walking and other tools to your excavation toolkit. Know which tool works best to jump start you toward your success.

Throughout his lifetime, W. Clement Stone studied how the mind works. He read extensively and as editor wrote about what he knew worked in his ***Success Unlimited*** magazine. Why not consider trying some of his techniques that enabled him to succeed beyond even his own best expectations? You will discover these tools in his book ***The Success System That Never Fails***. Why not use them yourself if they work? Otherwise, if your only tool is a hammer, expect the results that you have always received from hammering away!

Seed of Thought

The Success System That Never Fails
by W. Clement Stone

Magic Seed 2

Friendship rates with love as one of life's most precious assets. But like every desirable thing, friendship isn't free. There's a price on it which depends on the nature of the individual with whom you enjoy this coveted relationship.

–NAPOLEON HILL

Dear Readers:

It is said that inside each of us, we hold an eternal spring or vision of life that awakens newness in us daily if we choose to condition our minds in that direction. This is a good precursor to thoughts colored with a Positive Mental Attitude.

Many people get a renewed hold on life when spring finally rolls around. Warmer weather is anticipated, gardens are planned, seeds are ordered, and a person can be consoled with the thought that "this too shall pass" as the remnants of the last snowstorm melt away. And, we all know that February 14 is a day designed for friends–romantic or otherwise. Just relive the anticipation you felt in grade school and high school when that valentine was sent to you by someone special. Those acknowledgements made us bask in the glow of extra love and attention. We felt that special excitement combined with perhaps a little embarrassment too. But, wasn't it something to anticipate? You can be certain that it was.

Today does not have to be any different. You can email a friend, send a card, pick up the phone, write a short handwritten note, record a greeting, send a gift or flowers, and just make someone's day extra special. You receive by giving, and it is said that the aroma of flowers stays on the hands of the giver after the bouquet has been presented. What a karmic thought!

Friendships that are lasting relationships can help us through tough times. Whenever a friend is depressed due to any number of reasons, good friends help transfer the negative attention to some positive goal. The real prescription for easing depression is to do something–anything–simply because in the "doing" the mind can only harbor one thought. When you are thinking about being depressed, you are increasing the feelings of depression. Friends can recognize this and assist the individual in doing something other than stoking negative emotions. We attract what we focus on.

Napoleon Hill suggests going the extra mile, cultivating a pleasing personality, taking personal initiative, and following the Golden Rule as methods for helping others. When we are on the giving end, our lives take a turn for the positive and when we are on the receiving end, our lives turn toward the positive too. How can we lose?

So, go out and buy a box of bright red and white valentines today and address each one to a friend. Tell this person what their special friendship means to you. Usually, this can be said in a few sentences. Next, deliver those cards and see how the atmosphere lights up without adding anything but a few words. Words visually sparkle in someone's eyes when they read a sincere compliment. Do it now. Make friendship grow by being a friend! Tomorrow might be too late!

Seed of Thought

You Can Work Your Own Miracles
by Napoleon Hill

Magic Seed 3

When a person is struggling for recognition and advancement, seldom does he find anyone to give him a boost. But once he makes the grade, people stand in line to offer him help.

–NAPOLEON HILL

Dear Readers:

Let me remind you that whether you think you can or you think you can't you are correct. Many leaders have internalized this sentiment and when facing defeat even multiple times they consciously know that if they accept the current defeat and acknowledge it as final, they then become failures. Failure only happens if you allow it to happen and accept it as such.

By building self-confidence, self-esteem, and a positive mental attitude, we begin to arm ourselves against predicted failures. If we allow the failure mentality to creep surreptitiously into our thinking, we become entangled in the thought. The more we consider it, the harder failure's hold is to break. But, if we get up, shake ourselves off, and say "bring it on" then we look failure in the eye and challenge it to give its best shot at bringing us down. Nowhere does it say that when someone pronounces us a failure that we must accept the title. We are always told that where there is life there is hope. A failure mentality is only one way of thinking. There is another, and that is a success mentality.

Besides reading ***Think and Grow Rich*** and ***Law of Success*** for lessons on comebacks, read Viktor Frankl's ***Man's Search for Meaning***. This single book is the epitome on what holding a positive mental attitude can do for a person. Little do we realize that attitudes can extend or end our lives. Dr. Frankl has proven that attitudes do make a difference, and the difference results in the lives that we live. Do yourself a favor, and read this small book. Everything will be placed in the proper perspective when you do.

As you construct your positive mental attitude, don't forget to use the very best building supplies. Settle for nothing less than top grade materials. Keep in mind durability and appearance. Never whitewash something when it can be manufactured under the highest specifications. You are the perfect end result. Ask yourself, "Am I not worth the time devoted to the construction of **me**?" Sure you are...now let's go shopping for those perfect attitude building materials!

By the way, did you write those valentine notes last week? You won't see results until you put out some effort. In Emerson's words, "Do the thing and you will have the power." Do it now!

Seed of Thought

Man's Search for Meaning
by Viktor E. Frankl

Magic Seed 4

Whether ailing or not, I know of nothing that will bring peace of mind and sound health more quickly than the habit of counting one's blessings and recognizing them in a prayer of gratitude.

–NAPOLEON HILL

Dear Readers:

Dr. Hill states: "If you think you're sick, you are." How often do you allow yourself to focus on your illness rather than your health? When you are feeling fine and nothing ails you, do you give thanks to Infinite Intelligence for your well-being as Dr. Hill suggests? Do you require your Prince of Sound Health to keep your physical body healed and efficient at all times? To some, these actions may seem like mind games, however, today we know that our mind/body connection rules our health. Before going to sleep suggest to your subconscious mind that you will wake up healthy, happy, and terrific. With this command firmly stated and envisioned in your mind's eye, your subconscious mind will work while you sleep to make this a reality. No, it usually doesn't happen overnight, nor is it 100% predictable, but the success rate is higher than if you don't do it and it costs nothing but a positively directed thought as you drift off to sleep. As people who believe in self-help motivational literature, isn't it just common sense to practice what we preach?

When conducting seminars, I advocate various types of tools for personal development. I encourage participants to use these tools for increased effectiveness. I demonstrate their use, and I read testimonials from people who have benefited from using a specific technique. However, when I start to slip it is not because I am unaware of the techniques, it is because I don't use them! Once I begin again, my effectiveness goes up and yours will too. Reading cookbooks does not produce a gourmet dinner, armchair traveling doesn't give us the up close and personal experience, nor does reading self-help books transform us into little Napoleon Hills. We must take what we acquire and use it! The magic ingredients are lockstep actions that we take systematically one right after the other. And, no cheating! You can't skip steps and achieve the outcome that you dream about. You must place one foot in front of the other and march onward to your destiny. You can do it if you think you can.

Seed of Thought

Grow Rich With Peace of Mind
by Napoleon Hill

Magic Seed 5

Every ship in a fleet must make contact with the flagship at regular stated hours, whether or not there is anything to report.

–NAPOLEON HILL

Dear Readers:

Do you wonder why friends have stopped calling or connecting with you? Could it be that maybe you yourself broke the "contact" chain? Contacts are essential in all our lives. We communicate with family, co-workers, and others on a daily basis, however, those out-of-sight individuals are too often out-of-mind. We would do well to remember basic rules of etiquette with friends and everyone else. Here are ten things that are worth considering when dealing with another person:

1. When addressing an email or letter, begin with the person's name–even if it is a nuisance. People respond best when they read or hear their name being used.
2. Plan regular contact. When a person you consider a friend is at a distance, at least monthly if not weekly make a contact by phone, letter, email or personal visit.
3. Thank them for contacting you. Say, "It's good to hear from you. I missed your notes."
4. When you are with the friend in person, devote your attention to the friend. Turn off the cell phone and stay focused on the person you are with. An hour lunch meeting will not cause you to miss too many contacts, and it might save a very important one. Don't sandwich them in between another meeting or event. This is rude.
5. Express gratitude for something the friend has gone out of the way to do for you. Don't just expect it. When people give, and are not acknowledged for the giving the

wise person stops doing what doesn't work. Reciprocity in giving only occurs when it is a two way street.

6. As a giver, don't expect anything in return–but do expect acknowledgment. When someone gives you a gift, it is not the generosity that need be returned in dollars and cents, but rather the experience of giving something the person would value.
7. Put your feelings for the friend down in writing. That way, the friend can view it as a document that certifies that they are in your friendship file cabinet and you want them to stay there.
8. If the friend is unable to respond due to illness or has another valid reason, do not quit communicating. Keep the lines open in the hope that you will get a response when the person is able to give you one.
9. Think of the person before yourself and put their needs ahead of your own. Let's say, you see an article or a job posting that might be of interest to your friend, send it along–if appropriate–with a little note that states: "I thought that this might be of interest to you."
10. Finally, don't think for your friend. Don't prescribe a "you should do list," and don't work to persuade them to change. Most likely, they know their shortcomings and, unless requested, they do not need you to give them unasked for help. It is never appreciated.

If you sense that maybe you might be guilty of not following some of the points mentioned above, you could be at a loss for friends when you need them most.

Better get out there and start renewing those friendship merit badges!

Seed of Thought

Keys to Success:
The 17 Principles of Personal Achievement
by Napoleon Hill

Magic Seed 6

The successful person has learned that "whatever the mind of man can conceive and believe the mind of man can achieve." And this person keeps on keeping on until he converts his stumbling blocks into stepping stones. He knows that with every adversity comes the seed of an equivalent benefit.

–NAPOLEON HILL

Dear Readers:

If our belief is strong, our outcomes will be strong too. Believing in something with our heart and soul tends to make it happen. Just by affirming that you can do something, you are much closer to actually making it happen in your life. Dr. Hill states the formula for success simply in three words: Conceive, Believe, Achieve!

Conceive begins the process. It is an invitation to dream and to envision whatever it is we would like to manifest in our life. It might be looked upon as simple daydreaming or imagining by some and that is okay for a start. Allowing our fantasy to play out in our mind's eye is a good beginning process for later manifestation in the physical world. Conception is the very beginning of the birthing process, and it is essential in order to achieve whatever outcome that we set our sights on for the future.

Believe is stage two of the process. This is where the creative juices are turned up a notch and we begin to align our emotions with the desire. We not only imagine the outcome but we captivate our attention by adding the white heat of emotion to the mix and thereby ignite a flame that begins as a spark but grows into a bonfire of belief. Head and heart become one as we move toward manifesting our goal in the physical world. It can now be both clearly seen and felt, and the final logical step will enable us to achieve the intended outcome.

Achieve is the final stage of the process. Action is taken to ensure that the goal is drawn into the physical realm of our world and step by step we are led to the creation of whatever we envisioned at the onset. This is a critical stage, because many people never combine the action with the thought to create the doing. Without action on our part nothing will materialize. The achievement process is contingent on action taken. No action taken–no results seen–even if the vision is sharp and the belief is heartfelt, without action there will be no completion of the cycle.

Conception, gestation, and birth are the sequential process for the continuation of life on this planet. Ideas follow the same format, but they are not as easily seen because of their mental and spiritual components. But, an idea whose time has come will be seen in the physical world as the result of the actions that have been taken to produce it. At one point in Dr. Hill's career, a man in the audience approached him and told him that he could have written ***Think and Grow Rich***. As evidence of this fact, he reached into his coat pocket and pulled out notes that testified to his research. Dr. Hill acknowledged the fact that other people did similar research and believed in their project too, but it was only he that carried out the action part and actually wrote the book! As Dr. Hill so wisely knew, the proof is in the doing not in the intending. Remember that.

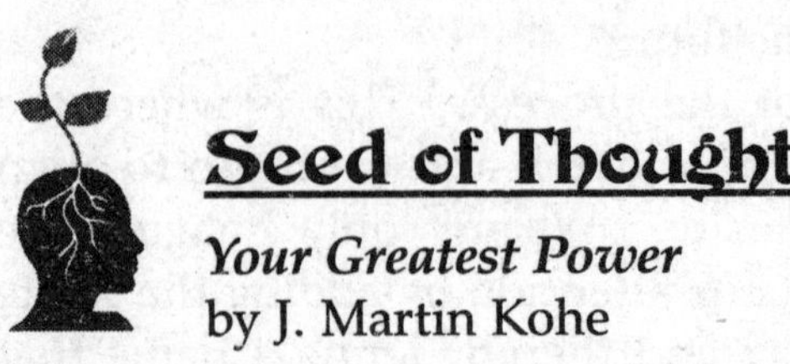

Your Greatest Power
by J. Martin Kohe

Magic Seed 7

If you can't do great things yourself, remember that you can do small things in a great way.

–NAPOLEON HILL

Dear Readers:

From an early age we are challenged by parents, teachers, relatives, ministers, and sometimes even friends to live up to our potential. Slogans promoting perfection and excellence seem to bombard us daily. Whether we are becoming better educated, professionally more astute, or an improved version of our former selves, we soon find that in the game of advancement it is the little things that make a profound difference. Generosity is often overlooked and underrated, but it can be one of those little things that make a big difference for you in the here and now.

W. Clement Stone frequently tells us to be generous. We may ask ourselves how simply being generous in small or large ways can elevate our lives. Thomas Moore has an idea that may relate. He states: "It's my conviction that slight shifts in imagination have more impact on living than major efforts at change." Consider that more thinking may not be the answer, but more action might be! Action contributes to creating more beneficial insights that may have gone unnoticed while we were busy thinking–i.e., allowing random thoughts to continually flow through our mind. Insights, not random thoughts, could change our lives because insights promote attitudinal change and hopefully promote better actions.

For example, if you have a habit you want to change you might research the internet for reasons as to why this habit is harmful. All the information could be at your fingertips, but you still persist in allowing the habit to control you. However, when the habit becomes too costly to maintain, a shift in the imagination occurs that opens wide a different path for you to follow. Perhaps you could pursue another habit that would be more beneficial–maybe a hobby instead of an addiction. Without first trying something on for size, we would never know what style suits us.

W. Clement Stone implies that we should give to get. This sounds almost the opposite of what we have been taught about not being selfish or self-serving. But, hold on a minute. Why shouldn't we reap what we sow? If it is good to give, it is also good to get. The error in thinking comes about when we expect equal and reciprocal action from the person we bestow the gift upon. This is not how it works. A circle of reciprocity is created by our generosity and our gift will come back to us from people and places known or unknown–no one is certain as to the future outcome. It cannot be predicted. That's the beauty of it. Goodness surfaces when it is least expected and that makes it all the more beautiful and timely for those of us who are storing up these treasures. Take some time today, be generous, and store up treasures for when you may need them the most. And, as the quote states: "Goodness and mercy shall follow me all the days of my life." Read W. Clement Stone's ***Believe and Achieve*** for his personal ideas on generosity.

Seed of Thought

Believe and Achieve
by W. Clement Stone

Magic Seed 8

Analysis of men and women in the upper brackets of success, in a variety of callings, reveals the astounding fact that each individual attained success in almost exact proportion to the adversities and defeats which had been met with and overcome.

–NAPOLEON HILL

Dear Readers:

March is the month of green, of four-leaf-clover wishing, and pots of gold at the end of the rainbow. It is also a convenient month for reassessing our New Year's Resolutions and seeing if we have stayed the course. Without a goal, we have no direction or gauge of accomplishment. Goals assist us in designing a purpose with a plan. Goals also take commitment and courage.

As we look to spring with a feeling of possibility in all that is good, let us once again reflect on what can freeze us in our journey toward success, the six basic fears. Dr. Hill explains each fear succinctly, yet effectively, in the final chapter of ***Think and Grow Rich*** and reminds us that truly we have nothing to fear but fear itself. Dr. Hill states: "fears are nothing more than states of mind. One's state of mind is subject to control and direction."

In summary, here are the six basic fears as defined by Dr. Hill and named in their most common appearance:

1. THE FEAR OF POVERTY. The mind attracts that which it dwells upon. The persons who condition their minds for the acceptance of poverty by fearing it and expecting it to be with them always will never be its master. The successful person conditions his mind for

financial success by deciding how much money he desires and keeping his mind fixed on this sum until he creates ways and means of getting it. You can't think in terms of poverty and hope to become financially independent.

2. THE FEAR OF CRITICISM: The major reason why so few people become top-ranking successes is their fear of what "they" will say if new and advanced ideas are adopted. Criticism can be of great benefit to the person who will use it to carefully analyze himself to determine how much of the criticism is accurate. Resentment of criticism is a sure way to tie one to a low station in life. The person who is headed toward success in the upper brackets of achievement welcomes honest criticism. He often pays high salaries to professionals who do just this. Honest criticism always is beneficial to the person who accepts it as an inspiration for self-improvement.
3. THE FEAR OF THE LOSS OF LOVE. This basic fear is at the bottom of most cases of jealousy. More often than not it has no real justification. But, justified or not, it is a sure killer of success opportunities.
4. THE FEAR OF ILL HEALTH. The doctors have a sixty-four-dollar word for this fear which is responsible for a large portion of their work. It is "hypochondria"—imaginary illness. Sound physical or mental health cannot exist with the individual who lives, talks and think in terms of ailments.
5. THE FEAR OF OLD AGE. The successful person transmutes this fear into a priceless benefit by recognizing that the Creator has wisely arranged for all individuals to trade their youth for priceless experience. The fact that a large majority of the greater successes of the world were attained by men and women who had passed the age of fifty should help anyone to master this fear and divert it to beneficial ends.
6. THE FEAR OF DEATH. This is the "grandfather" of all fears. The successful person properly relates himself to

this fear by accepting it as inevitable. He keeps himself so busy in his chosen calling that he has no time to devote to trying to solve the riddle of the hereafter. He leaves this to those who make it a profession.

So, as spring beckons us on to new journeys in life, close the door on fear and chart your course on the fearless road to success. And, may the luck of the Irish be with you and guide you all the way!!!!

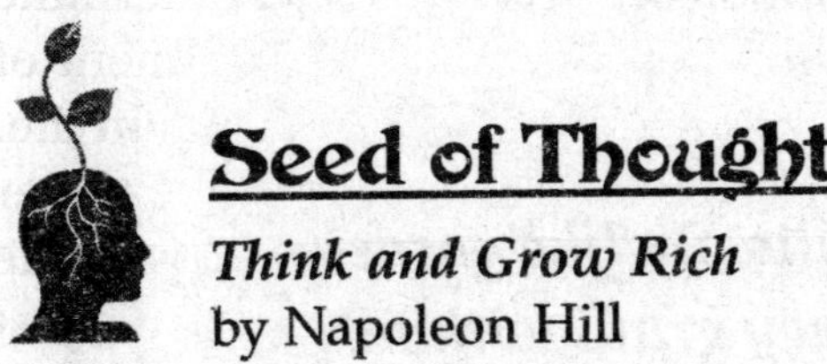

MORE SEEDS FOR SUCCESS

by Napoleon Hill

Human faults are like garden weeds. They grow without cultivation and soon take the place if they aren't thinned out.

Magic Seed 9

There is one human being on whom one can depend, without disappointment, in time of adversity, and this is one's self.

–NAPOLEON HILL

Dear Readers:

Napoleon Hill states that Faith and a Positive Mental Attitude are twin brothers. As we prepare for the coming of spring, and other events that mark the transition from adversity to hope, it is good to reflect on the advantages of defeat that Hill notes:

- Defeat speaks in a language that people of every tongue understand.
- It may have the effect of supplanting vanity and arrogance with humility of the heart.
- May cause one to acquire the habit of taking self-inventory.
- Lead to the development of a stronger will power.
- Break up undesirable relationships with others.
- Lead one into the deeper wells of sorrow.

These characteristics make us reflect on our need for cycles in our life that can and do cause us to reflect upon the circumstances and then to renew or reinvent ourselves for improved future outcomes.

Why not consider times of adversity and renewal in your life right now? Considering Dr. Hill's list, take a few moments now and recall the benefits that arose out of the adversities that you have experienced. This is getting to the kernel or seed of an equal or greater benefit that Hill discusses. Sometimes it takes fortitude to unearth these benefits and you may experience a long gestation period, but they are there nonetheless. And, when you decide to rebound and make the best of what has happened, I bet you will come out smelling like a rose every time!

Seed of Thought

Success Through a Positive Mental Attitude
by W. Clement Stone and Napoleon Hill

Magic Seed 10

First, all achievements, all successes and all desires begin with a clear mental image of one's goal—a definite picture of what you desire from life. Unless you know where you want to go, how can you get there?

–NAPOLEON HILL

Dear Readers:

When Napoleon Hill talks about the Guideposts to Success he means the 17 success principles that he uncovered during his lifetime of research. It is good to reflect on each of these principles as he often does in his writings. But, it is even better to consider how these success traits apply to us in our day-to-day activities. Are we reading about them or are we applying them? As Mark Twain states, the difference could be as diverse as that between a lightning bug and lightning. Ask yourself, which would you rather be? If your answer is the lightning that illuminates the sky and causes observers to sit up and take notice, then you need to be incorporating these traits into your daily actions. How else do you expect to sparkle?

It doesn't take much effort to start applying the 17 principles but you must do so daily and with foresight. Perhaps you can make a checklist of the principles much like a mini report card, and evaluate your progress daily. Keep a record for a month, and remind yourself to use all the principles—not just the ones you are good at. Begin with the Big Four as Hill terms them—Definiteness of Purpose, Mastermind Alliance, Applied Faith and Going the Extra Mile. Next add a few more that you decide to adopt for the day or the week. This is strength training, and in our classes we do what is called a PMA–EKG. You will soon get the idea. As we measure our heart rate for physical health, we should also measure our PMA rate for success health. Give it a try and I don't doubt that it will make a difference in your success quota. We all know that thoughts are things and what you think about you become. So, get busy with making the principles observable and measurable in your life. Therein lays the real difference. Remember the story of Jack and the Beanstalk? When planted, his magic seeds grew all the way to heaven. Yours can too! Success all begins with a single seed of thought.

Seed of Thought

Keys to Positive Thinking
by Napoleon Hill & Michael J. Ritt

Directions for use:

Score yourself on your use of Dr. Hill's 17 Success Principles by plotting a dot on the graph connected to your percentage of use. When you finish the scoring, you will have 17 dots that are plotted on the graph. Next, turn the paper so that the principles are located across the top of the page. With a pen or pencil, connect the dots starting with number 1 (Definiteness of Purpose) and proceeding to number 17 (Cosmic Habitforce). Notice that what you have here now resembles an EKG or heart rate printout. This is your POSITIVE MENTAL ATTITUDE EKG or measure of success! One last thing. Circle your three "highest" points and pat yourself on the back. Good work! Next, circle your three "lowest" points and get busy working on these three first. It does little good to keep polishing the apples, but it will do a tremendous amount of good if you work to improve your lower traits. Do this weekly and improve your results. If you do not hit the target, it's not the target's fault, but your own! Improve your aim and improve your results one assessment at a time.

Personal Analysis Report

Percentage										Principle
10	20	30	40	50	60	70	80	90	100	
										1. Definiteness of Purpose
										2. Mastermind
										3. Applied Faith
										4. Going the Extra Mile
										5. Pleasing Personality
										6. Personal Initiative
										7. Positive Mental Attitude
										8. Enthusiasm
										9. Self-Discipline
										10. Accurate Thinking
										11. Controlled Attention
										12. Teamwork
										13. Learning from Adversity & Defeat
										14. Creative Vision
										15. Maintenance of Sound Health
										16. Budgeting Time and Money
										17. Cosmic Habitforce

More Seeds for Success

by Napoleon Hill

Hatred spreads like wild weeds in a garden, without cultivation. Love must be nursed and cultivated or it will perish of starvation.

Magic Seed 11

Success doesn't crown the person who sells himself short through lack of self-confidence. But it does favor the person who knows what he wants, is determined to get it, and frowns at the word impossible.

–NAPOLEON HILL

Dear Readers:

Napoleon Hill states that having self-confidence is essential to success. Without self-confidence it does not matter what skills a person possesses since he will be unable to translate these skills into a positive action plan and then complete it. Self-confidence involves accurate thinking, controlled attention, and self-discipline. Without these principles firmly planted in a person's character nothing much will happen. In order to develop self-confidence a person must be a calculated risk taker. Taking a known risk for an anticipated positive outcome is just a developmental way of gaining more and more self-confidence. Even if the risk does not turn out as anticipated, a person learns a great deal through the risk taking process. The biblical admonition "Know Thyself" is the basis of all growth and development in this character trait.

Self-confidence–what it is and what it is not:

Self-confidence is belief in yourself. It is not cockiness, role playing, or the trying on of different personalities to see if there is a fit.

Self-confidence is knowing who you are and cherishing the treasure. It is not about making a big splash, but rather making a big difference through the use of your gift.

Self-confidence is self-knowledge and belief in your

abilities. It is not about stress driven accomplishments, but rather a slow and ongoing development of your best qualities over time.

Self-confidence is about class, not ego.

Self-confidence is your personal aura of certainty that presents itself in overall composure. It is not a frenzied attempt to keep up; rather it is the internal knowing that you have already arrived.

Self-confidence is the utilization of common sense. It is not an accumulation of knowledge, but rather the use of internal wisdom that allows you to be the **"you"** that **you** were born to be.

When discussing self-confidence in class, I often ask students to browse through their early photo albums and select two or three pictures that display their evident inborn self-confidence. These are photos with natural poses where you are caught off-guard enjoying life. Find two or three. Examine them closely for the spirit within the child, and then ask yourself if self-confidence was present and visible. How did it feel? Have you maintained it? Or, is it lost or hidden under self-doubt? Isn't it time to bring it out once again, polish it up, and display it for the world to see? Seek the treasure and realize that the magic was inside you all the time. What are you waiting for? Be a positive risk-taker and reap the benefit of finding your self-confidence waiting right inside you!

Seed of Thought

You Can
by George Matthew Adams

Magic Seed 12

The subconscious has one very peculiar trait, it believes everything one tells it, and acts accordingly. It not only believes and acts upon one's spoken words, but more astounding still, it believes in and acts upon one's thoughts; especially those thoughts which are highly emotionalized with either faith or fear.

–NAPOLEON HILL

Dear Readers:

Reading is to the mind what food is to the body. It is a form of mental nourishment that none of us can do without. Reading opens up our self-confidence by providing us with communication tools that connect us to others. It gives us topics of conversation, areas of interest, and in-depth information on current events and historical happenings. Reading bridges the past and the future, it allows us to gain knowledge in the comfort of our own home, and it sharpens our minds because it is an active not passive practice.

If we read actively, reading can change us through interaction with the text. Thoughts, ideas, opinions, attitudes, beliefs, and values are all influenced and cultivated through reading. Words carry heavy weight when they are both spoken and written. The written word has permanence, much like a contract, that can be timeless. Dr. Hill states: "The spoken word leaves impressions, the printed word leaves tracks."

Reading is like any other exercise. The more you practice, the more proficient you become. In order to be an expect reader, you must read frequently if not daily, and improve your ability by selecting works that are just a little above your current reading level. Much like interval training, the reader must read material he is comfortable with for pleasure, but next challenge himself with a text that is written at a level just beyond the level that is easy to read.

Readers gain self-confidence as they master the art. To read with comprehension is to acquire knowledge that is useful in life. Dr. Hill was a strong advocate of reading and libraries. He felt that this was a credible way to acquire knowledge. Accurate Thinking is based on ideas that have been judged to be of value because they can be tested for their accuracy. Dr. Hill's "How do you know?" question most often can be substantiated through books. Remember too, it was Andrew Carnegie who funded libraries across the nation as his gift to the general public. Many of these libraries stand yet today as a visible testimony to Carnegie's generosity and foresight.

Books can teach a person how to build a home, prepare a meal, meditate, raise chickens, give a speech, form a mastermind alliance, and write books. All a person has to know in advance is how to locate a good book on the subject matter of interest. Once found, a book can open doors that advance careers and prepare the reader for the next step. When Napoleon Hill's step-mother tempted Napoleon with a typewriter in exchange for his six-shooter, she was supporting the notion that "Readers are Leaders." Give reading a try yourself and see if you don't gain in self-confidence because now you have something valuable to share. Be careful. Reading as a form of exercise can be addictive. Remember to exercise your mind because it is your most valuable tool in your success tool kit. Read any good books lately?

Seed of Thought

Making Miracles

by Arnold Fox, M.D. & Barry Fox, Ph.D

Magic Seed 13

You can be a man with a grievance or a man with a message; you can be a BUILDER or a DESTROYER, but make sure of this, that you can no more tear down without in turn being torn down, than you could sow wild mustard and reap a harvest of oats.

–NAPOLEON HILL

Dear Readers:

Do you believe in the Golden Rule? Does "Do unto others as you would have others do unto you" reverberate through your entire being and give you goose bumps when you get it right? When you sense someone's need, do you strive to fill it or overlook it? Therein, as Shakespeare would say "is the rub." The difference in what we do comes from our rationale for doing it. Selfish motives are not applicable because the ego is the central focus and beneficiary. Motives that acknowledge and embrace others are inclusive not exclusive. Dr. Hill endorses applying the Golden Rule by becoming a builder, not a destroyer. The mission of the Golden Rule is to build up not tear down.

Andrew Carnegie was a builder. During his lifetime he provided the funding for libraries to be built nationwide. When we consider the magnitude of Carnegie's generosity in giving away 90% of his accumulated wealth in grants for libraries in the United States, we begin to appreciate the unparalleled generosity of this Scotsman. In Indiana alone, 155 separate communities were recipients of Carnegie's love for reading and for the buildings that were dedicated to the housing of books. Lovingly dubbed the Patron Saint of Libraries, Andrew Carnegie is touching lives yet today because of his profound philanthropy.

Napoleon Hill was strongly influenced by Andrew Carnegie. Perhaps his ideas concerning the Golden Rule and Going the Extra Mile have a positive correlation with life as Carnegie modeled it for the young Hill. Seeing the positive uses that wealth could be put to, Dr. Hill began to uncover the true riches of life. Isn't it ironic that a cub reporter tells the story of the world's wealthiest man, and his subsequent philosophy of success immortalizes the man as much as Carnegie's monetary gift to the world? It has been said, life is strange. Hill states that there is a Law of Compensation in effect universally. Simply put, this is the law of Karma. In colloquial language, it is stated most efficiently as "what goes around comes around." Now might be a good time to ask yourself, what type of energy are you sending out? Are you a builder or a destroyer? Watch out, because it could easily come back around to diminish you or to uplift you! And it is all because of the little word–**do**. What you **do** is what you **get** over time. Hill refers to two envelopes that life hands to us on the moment of our birth. One labeled REWARDS and the other labeled PENALTIES. Which one will you open? What you **do** determines your fate.

Seed of Thought

The Wisdom of Andrew Carnegie
by Napoleon Hill

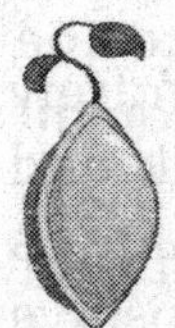

Magic Seed 14

Plant the seed of service that is right in quality and quantity, then watch what happens when you have established the reputation of being a person who always renders better service than that which is paid for.

–NAPOLEON HILL

Dear Readers:

Both Napoleon Hill and W. Clement Stone continually remind us to put our wishes, hopes, dreams, and desires down on paper. Why is this act an important step in the accumulation of riches? The answer is simple to understand. When we put something in writing, in essence we are creating a contract with ourselves. We are telling our subconscious mind through the writing process that we are serious about these desires and want to begin to see them manifested in our everyday lives. Also, in conceptualizing our desires we begin the visualization process that imprints on our subconscious mind exactly what goals we are working toward. Next, we generate a burning desire tied to the goal and that is exactly when applied faith enters into the total picture. We want it to happen, we can see it happening in our mind's eye, we upgrade our desire to a burning desire, and then we refuse to accept the possibility of it not happening. This assurance of our chosen outcome activates applied faith, and then the only result possible is a positive result. Applied Faith is the doorway to Infinite Intelligence and this doorway exists in our subconscious mind.

How can you prove that writing is important for goal setting? Why not start in a simple way by writing personal letters to family members, friends, and business associates?

These letters should be informal, friendly, to the point, and offer encouragement in a particular field of interest to the recipient. By doing this, you crystallize your own thought process and also generate goodwill. This goodwill activates the Law of Compensation and the Law of Attraction in your behalf. How can you lose?

IDEA ONE:
Napoleon Hill reminds us that:

Love is the warp and the woof of all the riches of life. It embellishes all riches and gives them the quality of endurance, evidence of which may be revealed by cursory observation of all who have acquired material riches but have not acquired love.

IDEA TWO:
He also states that:

The habit of Going the Extra Mile leads to the attainment of that spirit of love, for there can be no greater expression of love than that demonstrated through service rendered unselfishly for the benefit of others.

Letter writing can help us incorporate Napoleon Hill's two ideas for our personal benefit.

Hill's business partner, W. Clement Stone, used letter writing to his personal advantage during his long lifetime.

Stone states:

To write—you must think You are what you think. *When you write a letter, you crystallize your thinking on paper.* ***Your imagination is developed by recollecting the past, analyzing the present, and perceiving the future.*** *The more often you write, the more you take pleasure in writing. By asking questions, you, as the writer, direct the mind of the recipient into desired channels. You can make it easy for him to respond to you—thus, when he does, he becomes the writer and you the recipient.*

The receiver of the letter you write is forced to think in terms of—you. His thinking follows the pattern of your written, expressed ideas. If your letter is well thought out, both his reason and his emotions can be directed along desired paths.

This is powerful material to know because just by taking pen in hand, you can direct the outcome, or at least sway the outcome, of many events. Do not be afraid to express yourself in this manner. If you are still shy about putting pen to paper in corresponding with your family or associates, here are 10 simple steps to get you started.

1. Be a "good finder" within your family. When someone does something "good," notice it and write a complimentary note indicating that you acknowledge it.
2. Thank someone for doing something for you that made a difference in your life. It could be a letter to a schoolteacher, a spiritual advisor, a friend, family member or associate. The key thing is to acknowledge the fact and thank the person for it in writing. This makes it official.
3. Get in the daily habit of sending "good news" emails to individuals who may be feeling forgotten. Just simply say, "Glad you are in my life."
4. Send at least one written note per day to a different person each day. This is not a big time investment, but at the end of each month, you will have accumulated 30 days of goodwill from 30 different people.
5. Read Emerson's *Law of Compensation* Essay and truly begin to understand why focusing on the goodness in life brings more of the same back to you.
6. Don't forget about yourself. Buy a journal and write yourself a note of encouragement, a "love" letter, and a good news report. Be specific and notice the good things in your life. Also, ask for more.
7. Remember not to leave out Infinite Intelligence either. Write a note of gratitude to God indicating what you are truly grateful for in your life and sign it and date it.
8. Treat yourself to some new paper and pens or pencils.

Make writing a pleasure, not a chore.

9. Organize your address book, so that when the mood strikes you to write, you have the information at your fingertips.
10. Keep a running log of what happens as a result of your writing project. Give it a month to cycle back around to you. You will be amazed at the good that you do and more importantly the good it does for you. Practice the self-starter: Do It Now!

Remember, when you express yourself on paper in letter format, you immortalize yourself through the printed word. Even though we die, our written words can last forever. How often do you look at a note, a signature, or a recipe penned by a loved one who has passed on and think of them fondly? Our society is one of written contracts. When something is written and signed, it means more. Give more this month, write a letter and wait for the response. You won't be disappointed.

Seed of Thought

How to Become a Mental Millionaire
by J. Martin Kohe and Judith Williamson

Magic Seed 15

Single-handed no man can accomplish enough to cause much of a stir; but, through allied effort Rockefeller became the world's richest man, Henry Ford has astounded the world and put the most learned men to shame by comparison, James J. Hill got up from the telegraph key and became the greatest builder of railroads, and George Washington carved his name at the head of the list of immortal patriots.

–NAPOLEON HILL

Dear Readers:

In the introduction to the May, 1954 issue of *Success Unlimited,* W. Clement Stone quotes Napoleon Hill as he states: "Success is getting what you want out of life without violating the rights of others."

He goes on to add, "What you want is up to you. Not everyone cares to be an Eisenhower or an Edison. Not all choose to pay the costly price of becoming and remaining famous. To many the riches of life are those tiny triumphs of day-to-day living and loving which build up to a crescendo of the beautiful, well-spent life."

Just what are the riches of life? Napoleon Hill defines the Twelve Riches of Life as follows:

1. A Positive Mental Attitude
2. Sound Physical Health
3. Harmony in Human Relationships
4. Freedom from Fear
5. The Hope of Achievement
6. The Capacity for Faith
7. Willingness to Share One's Blessings
8. A Labor of Love

9. An Open Mind on All Subjects
10. Self-Discipline
11. The Capacity to Understand People
12. Financial Security

It may be worth noticing that Dr. Hill places financial security on the bottom of the list. In defining success he states: "Whatever success you attain will be attained through the proper use of your mind. Your physical, muscle power counts for *nothing*. Your mind power counts for *everything*." And, he adds: "Generally speaking, a man has succeeded when he has acquired all that he needs for his physical and spiritual well-being without having trespassed on the rights of his fellowmen." As an example, note that Hitler did not achieve the ultimate success he desired. Simply stated, he violated the rights of his fellowman, and therefore due to the Law of Compensation he was not entitled to any reward.

In summary, Stone continues, "But whether success to you means the discovery of a new element–the breaking of a sales or production records–the acquisition of bigger and better houses, cars or incomes–the creation of art, music or literature for all time–the growing of the perfect rose–or the loving smile from your cherished child–we believe that your success can be unlimited."

Why not take a few minutes right now to reflect on your personalized definition of success? In a few short, descriptive sentences like W. Clement Stone wrote in the above paragraph, describe what success means to you in all the intricate detail. See if your definition matches up with what you have in your life right now. If not, why not? Thinking can make it so. Thoughts are things. Put thoughts to your best use in making success happen in your life the exact way you envision it.

Seed of Thought

A Treasury of Success Unlimited
by Og Mandino

Magic Seed 16

I will not engage in any business or sport that implies fraud, cruelty or injustice to any living thing.

–NAPOLEON HILL

Dear Readers:

Each of us is responsible for making a difference in our lives and in the lives of those around us. Therefore, each of us is a potential teacher and needs to be aware of this role. All teachers model behaviors, intentional or not, and students replicate those behaviors, good or bad.

In motivational talks, seminar presenters have "teasers" that get people's attention. Anthony Robbins uses the fire walk. People are intrigued and enroll for his seminars because they want to say that they have navigated the red-hot coals without a single blister. Well, unfortunately, Napoleon Hill left us no gimmicks. The closest thing to a "teaser" that could be aligned to Dr. Hill's Philosophy of Success would be a hand held mirror. If we agree to the fact that there is one aspect that we cannot afford to overlook when giving ourselves a success makeover and that is ourselves, then the hand help mirror serves as a good prop. The mirror becomes a metaphor for introspection and introspection is the one crucial aspect that develops our success consciousness. Dr. Hill states: "You do not see your real self when you look into a mirror. You only see the house in which your real self lives."

Why a mirror? Well, to really see something we must observe, and to analyze something we must look within before we can conjecture about what is to happen without. As you gaze into the mirror, I would like you to consider these four characteristics that underscore personal development.

First, a renewed self calls for checks on personal

performance and individual perception. To cite a passage from President Clinton's inaugural address in 1997, President Clinton states: "And once again, we have resolved for our time a great debate over the role of government. Today we can declare: Government is not the problem, and government is not the solution. We–the American people–we are the solution." Here comes the mirror part–look within for the answers!!!

Second, we need to profess action, not dialogue, when dealing with renewal. As teachers (and we all are), we need to know the progression of learning. Bloom identifies six "stairsteps" to learning. Beginning at ground level they are: knowledge, comprehension, application, analysis, synthesis and evaluation. Bloom indicates that to know a concept in all its intricate detail, one must progress actively through the stages of learning. Consider that application is midway up the ladder of learning and comes before the evaluation stage. Before we can formulate an educated opinion we must have some basis in real life experience, i.e., application. For example, Napoleon Hill states: "Opinions are the cheapest commodity on earth. Everybody has them." Here comes the mirror part–can you observe and measure yourself actively doing something? Or, is your best advice just an opinion, and not an educated one at that? Dr. Hill tells us to develop a plan and then work the plan. Can you catch yourself in your mirror working the plan by walking the talk?

Third, renewal screams for outcome. Are you on a diet, an exercise program, or a day-by-day spiritual reformation? Well, then, you expect results such as weight loss, a stronger body, and increased spirituality as you progress. If you don't know where you are going, any road will get you there. Obviously, you must have a plan to reach a destination. Working the plan creates a roadmap. If we know the direction we are going, subsequent steps in the right direction will get us there even if we only take one step at a time. Oliver Wendell Holmes Jr. states, "Where we stand is not as important as the direction in which we are moving." Here comes the mirror part–can you see yourself moving in the direction of your dream? If not, turn around.

Finally, success consciousness causes introspection coupled with ongoing personal assessment. "Ask not what your country can do for you, ask what you can do for your country" is an often heard quotation that still rings true. Have some fun with this. Try substituting your favorite noun–concrete or abstract–for country and hear how purposeful it sounds.

Ask not what your job can do for you,
ask what you can do for your job.

Ask not what your dreams can do for you,
ask what you can do for your dreams.

Ask not what your mother can do for you,
ask what you can do for your mother.

This little activity guides you toward creating a goal and a direction. It builds enthusiasm. It propels you to an outcome. Here comes the mirror part–see that star in the background? Hitch your wagon to it.

But, but, but, what else can I do? How do we become action-oriented in the process of developing our overall success capability? Here are a few fun suggestions:

1. Develop a personal ad campaign. Continually ask, "How am I doing?"
2. Display a positive mental attitude even when you are not positive.
3. Reflect an attitude of gratitude.
4. Look for evidence of good things sent to us by the Universe.
5. Document what you have DONE–visible activities–versus mental abstractions.
6. Hold up the mirror to your performance and ask yourself these questions:
   a. What is working?
   b. What is not working?
   c. What portion is observable?
   d. What portion is measurable?

e. Which one or ones of the above things are action-oriented?

Now, you have refocused and you can see the mirror images in a much clearer fashion. Throw out the drudgery and revitalize yourself by focusing on behaviors and outcomes. Remember the least action is worth far more than the greatest intention. Do not intend to act. Act. Ask people how you are doing. Listen to what is said, but recall you are only receiving someone else's opinion. Distill it for what it is worth. Do less and accomplish more. But, do it now.

Finding your definite major purpose requires that you uncover what you do best. Don't force interest where none exists. Intensify versus trivialize. Do only what is significant to you, but do it well. All Rosa Parks had to do was sit, but this action seated her in our nation's history. Just sit. Sounds wonderful. Think about it. One thought, one vibration, one idea can create a rippling effect that could change the course of the world.

Looking at ourselves promotes introspection. Acute observation serves as a catalyst for growth and development. When we look within, we promote movement beyond the problem toward the solution. When we look within, the significance of attitudes becomes apparent. When we look within, we uncover universal laws for success.

Address the mirror. Be committed to growth and development. You will be pleasantly surprised at what the mirror has in store for you during YOUR next state of YOUR union address.

Do good and good will come back to you. Always does, always will. It is the law of Cosmic Habitforce. To quote Dr. Hill:

> Take possession of your positive self and it will put you on the SUCCESS BEAM where you may ride triumphantly to whatever heights of achievement you desire.

Magic Seed 17

Education comes from within; you get it by struggle and effort and thought.

—NAPOLEON HILL

Dear Readers:

Having just completed our annual open house at the Napoleon Hill World Learning Center, I am still reeling from all the programs, speakers, and guests that we experienced. Whether the attendee was a participant or a presenter, each person made a valuable contribution to the wonderful outcome of the week. I would like to use this platform to publically compliment our speakers for their contribution. By highlighting a significant aspect of their presentation, you, the reader, can begin to see how each contributed to our Journey to Success.

Chino Martinez for his presentation on the labyrinth and its use as a transformative tool in personal growth. And, the physical construction of the labyrinth on campus grounds followed by the actual walking of the labyrinth with the intention of World Peace.

Fr. Robert Sipe for his availability for personal reflection and discussion for those seeking spiritual growth and development. Also, for his impromptu blessings before meals and of the labyrinth.

Mike Frain for his heartfelt and inspiring talk on learning from adversity and defeat. Although under treatment for cancer, Mike delivered his talk with the determination and stamina that demonstrate his remarkable PMA spirit.

Christina Chia for her openness in speaking on the topic of gratitude and how it raises a person to a higher level of spirituality and personhood. Coming all the way from Kuala Lumpur, Malaysia, Christina never fails to inspire us with her enthusiasm and her love for Dr. Hill's philosophy.

James Spooner for once again demonstrating the truth in Dr. Hill's statement–"Whatever the mind can conceive and believe, the mind can achieve." This statement is true for the past, the present, and the future. Mr. Spooner demonstrated how by focusing on our future as if it **IS** the **NOW**, we can create truth in advance, and a heaven on earth with one positive thought at a time.

Kelly King for his phenomenal talk on creative visioning that rises like a phoenix from the adversities of life. Kelly points out that this is not a natural reaction, but one that must be cultivated by looking for the seed of an equal or greater benefit within the adversity that one has just experienced.

Fred Wikkeling for his seminar on discerning the different personality types of individuals and how a person can best interact with and benefit from knowing about the various types. His little book "Look UP!" continues to inspire people with its simplistic yet powerful message of maintaining a positive mental attitude.

Richard Krasney for his financial planning advice coupled with the knowledge that everyone can be a philanthropist and make a profound difference by giving from one's gifts whether monetary or otherwise.

Dr. Judy Arcy for her real life discussion of creating a Mastermind Alliance and using illustrations from the Haka (a tribal dance) and the Koru (a fern-like plant) to demonstrate how this process works.

Jan Mahannah for involving the audience emotionally through song, storytelling, and dance as the journey for significance and success unfolds in a person's life. Also, for introducing us to the song "Beautiful People Awake."

Don Green for conducting the graduation ceremony for the Keys to Success class and sending the graduates onward to great accomplishments inspired by his Keynote Address on the 17 Principles of Success.

Jim Connelly for the sharing of his personal memories of Knute Rockne, Rudy, and Lou Holtz in preparation for the viewing of the play "Knute Rockne" at the Munster Center for the Performing Arts. Jim's lifelong embodiment of Hill's philosophy makes him a personification of the philosophy of success. He truly walks the talk.

For special guest **Dr. J. B. Hill** (Napoleon's grandson) for spending time with us at the open house and learning about our educational mission. His participation and support are a generous gift to us. Dr. Napoleon Hill would be honored to see his grandson follow so closely in his footsteps.

Ongoing kudos to our Executive Director **Don Green** and Board President **James Olson** for annually supporting and attending our Open House event.

Finally, a special "thank you" to **Chino Martinez, Alan (Guang) Chen**, and special assistant **Becky Jarvis** for doing all the behind the scenes work and preparation that enabled this event to happen so smoothly and so successfully.

It's important to note that these speakers, as well as twelve special ambassadors from Japan shared their time and talent with each of us. It is a wonderful thing to experience the people of the world coming together in harmony for a common, peaceful purpose. Truly, the mission of the Foundation to make the world a better place in which to live is happening one person at a time right here at the Napoleon Hill World Learning Center!

Seed of Thought

Success with People
by Cavett Robert

Magic Seed 18

The Counsel Table around which I gather, with these great men of the past each night, is an imaginary one, but the messages which they left behind them are real, and I am using this method of burning them deeply into my consciousness, that their influence may find its way into the pattern after which my character is being built.

–NAPOLEON HILL

Dear Readers:

Like the Cowardly Lion in the ***Wizard of Oz,*** most of us do not see ourselves as heroes. We feel faint of heart and seek the courage that we fear we lack. Courage is a trait that can only be built internally. Unless we are awarded a medal for all to see, we may not recognize courage in ourselves. Courage, like faith, is only useful when applied. Attempting to instill courage in another is pointless. It must be developed from within–either the seed is planted and grows or the field lies fallow. How then, does one cultivate courage, or any number of other worthy traits? Possibly, Dr. Hill gives us a clue in his use of the Imaginary Counselors.

Dr. Hill's imaginary counselors serve as a committee of advisors that provide information when asked. Since they were selected due to certain traits that Dr. Hill wanted to develop in his personality, they could never respond or react "out of character." For example, Abraham Lincoln could not make prejudicial statements because intolerance was not a part of his makeup. Emerson could not advocate "group think" when he held personhood is such high regard. The idea is that a person's values come to embody and then transform the person. Dr. Hill reminds us that "Thoughts are things." And, "What you think about, you become." Therefore, if you want to embody the value of being courageous, you need to study the acts of courageous people whose values align with yours or with those you want to acquire. That is why it is so essential to study the lives and biographies of those we wish to model. In reading about a person's life, you can acquaint yourself with their selfless acts and envision ways that you can grow your own personality by emulating them. Dr. Hill did exactly this as he prepared to write his classic works, ***Law of Success*** and ***Think and Grow Rich***. By interviewing over 500 people, Hill had ample sources to draw his conclusions from for his lifetime work.

Why not set aside some time today to research someone you wish to model? If living, you might share the fact that you admire a particular trait in this person's personality and ask them how they acquired it. If deceased, you might read a biography on the person. Examples are Napoleon Hill, Thomas Edison, Mother Teresa, Winston Churchill, Eleanor Roosevelt, Emily Dickinson, Shakespeare, Emerson, Thoreau, Vincent Van Gogh, Monet, and the list goes on and on. Just as in a fashion sense, you wear the dress that you wish to integrate into your personal look so too do you clothe your interior look. The style that counts in the long run is the style that you wear on the inside. Let your little light shine, and remember a candle is never diminished by sharing the flame, rather it can expand to illuminate the way for others. As Emerson reminds us, "Do the thing and you shall have the power." Success leaves tracks. Explore, discover the tracks, follow the road, and arrive at your destination. As Dorothy reminds us in the ***Wizard of Oz***, it was really that simple all along.

Seed of Thought

The Power of Your Subconscious Mind
by Dr. Joseph Murphy

Magic Seed 19

Time is the only priceless treasure in the universe!

—NAPOLEON HILL

Dear Readers:

Napoleon Hill's reflections on the nature and substance of Time are interesting. He appears to believe that Time is a variable in our character development that allows us the opportunity to play out our destiny. Dr. Hill might be suggesting that if given enough time a person may finally get it "right." I would concur as long as learning is also factored into the study. Added to the human experiment there must be an amount of learning that develops into wisdom for a transformation to occur. People do not change positively over time without additional catalysts.

I have known many people who grow like weeds, and also those who seem to be stunted or nipped in the bud. Hill often reminds us that the universe hates only two things: a vacuum and inactivity. Both are conducive to change because a vacuum is eventually filled by a personal choice or the choice of the universe, and inactivity produces changes that are a consequence of the inaction. For example, ever notice how a desktop does not remain uncluttered for long? Mail accumulates, notes appear, clutter arrives, and it seems as if it all has a mind of its own. You must work to keep your desktop, dining room table, cabinets, car trunk, and a variety of other things in order. It does not happen spontaneously. In fact, by doing nothing you do not postpone the inevitable, but actually accelerate the decline. That is where inaction enters the picture.

I also know people who believe that if they do not act

they are forestalling the inevitable. Nothing could be further from the truth. Inaction is a decision, and one that puts you in reverse. You decide to do nothing, and that is a decision. Not only does this stop you in your tracks, but because others choose to act differently they are moving forward and you are moving backward. See how the declining distance is created?

Time treats everyone the same, but the way you respect time demonstrates time's respect for you. It is interesting to view time from many perspectives, not just our own. In many instances it seems that time has passed in the blink of an eye. Something tells me that we all have that realization at critical points in our lives—births, graduations, marriages, and deaths are the typical times that cause people to pause and reflect. Therefore, let's use time to our best advantage. Respect it, don't waste it, and use it wisely because it can be over in an instant!

How are you using your time? Napoleon Hill asks this question, and he immediately reminds us that each of us has the same seconds, minutes, and hours in a day. No more, no less. Time treats everyone the same, but how we use the time we are given makes all the difference in the world to us!

Seed of Thought

Wake Up! You're Alive
Arnold Fox, M.D. & Barry Fox, Ph. D

Magic Seed 20

In the mad rush for glory and fame and dollars let us not forget the hand that rocks the cradle. We may not raise ourselves in the estimate of men, by honoring her as she is entitled to be honored, but, by doing so we are not apt to lower ourselves in the eyes of God.

–NAPOLEON HILL

Dear Readers:

Dr. Napoleon Hill always credited two people with placing him squarely on the path to success during his early years. The first was his step-mother, Martha, and the second was his sponsor, Andrew Carnegie. We often hear a great deal about Andrew Carnegie, but not as much about the equally influential step-mother. In later years, Hill stated that the death of his natural mother was a "blessing in disguise" because it allowed Martha to come into his life and encourage him to become a writer. Surely, Dr. Hill often wondered as he wrote where he would be without the positive change that Martha provided.

Martha arranged for Napoleon to own his first typewriter. In turn, this directly enabled him to discover that he had a knack for writing. Essentially, she saw something good in him and worked to bring it out. Educators who inspire students to look for talents inside themselves are gifted at doing this. As the former wife of an educator, Martha was an excellent student in the psychology of motivation herself.

Martha was the widow of a high school principal who not only challenged Napoleon to get on the "success beam," but did so for her new husband as well. Wanting to better her station in life, she refused to accept the status that her new marriage provided. Determined, she set her mind to making a licensed dentist out of Napoleon's father, and did so with the money she acquired from her first husband's death insurance. Convinced that something more was available to this young family in the way of success, Martha was committed to make it happen. Her burning desire caught hold in the family and she transformed them into what she first conceived and believed in her mind. All that the family had to do was put into action the vision she held before them. The achievement part was easy when the proper attitude was in place.

Dr. Hill often speaks of the critical difference mothers make in the lives of their children. He recognizes that without their vision, support, and endurance most of us would not be where we are today. Whether male or female, today each of us can be mother to an idea, a mother to encouragement, and a mother to recognition of a job well done. When we place ourselves in the capacity of a doer of simple things, of things that are done behind the scenes, of things that oftentimes go without recognition or reward, but are essential steps to what is to come after, we are the mother of invention, the mother referred to in Nature, and the mother who can turn the tide for one person or a class by charting the course for the future.

Mothers are visionaries. They see into the future. They challenge us to be everything that we were placed on earth to become. They do not settle for less than that which we are capable. Maybe that small, quiet voice within each of us really is our mother. Some say it is our conscience or innate knowledge of good and evil. But, surely if we asked our mother for advice, she would say the very same thing as that still, small voice within each of us. That's a comforting thought because whether living or deceased, our mother will always be with us to guide, motivate, and praise our accomplishments.

Why not take a moment today to thank someone young

or old who has "mothered" you on your life's journey? Acknowledge the important part that they play in your success. Say "thank you" as Dr. Hill did and you will feel the better for it.

And, personally, I would like to say "Thanks, Mom." You made a tremendous difference in my life! I am forever grateful.

Seed of Thought

Poems that Inspire You to Think and Grow Rich
by Napoleon Hill & Judith Williamson

MORE SEEDS FOR SUCCESS

by Napoleon Hill

Men who sow the seed of dissention always expect to reap a crop of something they didn't earn.

Magic Seed 21

Wherever there is work to be done you can find a chance to become a leader. It may be humble leadership, at first, but the leadership becomes a habit and soon the most humble leader becomes a powerful man of action and he is then sought for greater leadership.

–NAPOLEON HILL

Dear Readers:

I know many fathers that consistently go the extra mile for their children and the children of others too. So, as you practice being a good role model for those who look up to you, consider what both Dr. Hill and W. Clement Stone have stated about the ideas of leadership and raising children. Although taking different perspectives, each offers good suggestions when it comes to nurturing, mentoring, coaching, and modeling behaviors that would be good to emulate. No one said being a dad would be easy, and it is probably the most rewarding occupation you will ever have in life. Watching those you love grow and develop into global citizens with values consistent with positive beliefs that you hold dear, is payment enough for the long hours that you have contributed to their upbringing.

When I think of parenting, I like to consider the idea of not only giving children roots but also wings. Each is significant. Roots are for grounding and wings are for visioning. Without the fundamentals in place like food, clothing and shelter, the extraordinary aspects in life are hard to imagine. Likewise, without imagination life can become mundane and routine. Both grounding and visioning are essential elements that contribute to a life well lived.

Rudyard Kipling is a poet who has written a poem called "If." In this poem are elements of what makes a boy a man. The ideas are worth reflection. Although the poem is dedicated to a young man, the thoughts are applicable to young women as well. In short, Kipling characterizes what it takes to be a real winner in life.

IF

by Rudyard Kipling

If you can keep your head when all about you
Are losing theirs and blaming it on you,
If you can trust yourself when all men doubt you
But make allowance for their doubting too,
If you can wait and not be tired by waiting,
Or being lied about, don't deal in lies,
Or being hated, don't give way to hating,
And yet don't look too good, nor talk too wise:

If you can dream–and not make dreams your master,
If you can think–and not make thoughts your aim;
If you can meet with Triumph and Disaster
And treat those two impostors just the same;
If you can bear to hear the truth you've spoken
Twisted by knaves to make a trap for fools,
Or watch the things you gave your life to, broken,
And stoop and build 'em up with worn-out tools:

If you can make one heap of all your winnings
And risk it all on one turn of pitch-and-toss,
And lose, and start again at your beginnings
And never breathe a word about your loss;
If you can force your heart and nerve and sinew
To serve your turn long after they are gone,
And so hold on when there is nothing in you
Except the Will which says to them: "Hold on!"

If you can talk with crowds and keep your virtue,
Or walk with kings—nor lose the common touch,
If neither foes nor loving friends can hurt you;
If all men count with you, but none too much,
If you can fill the unforgiving minute
With sixty seconds' worth of distance run,
Yours is the Earth and everything that's in it,
And—which is more—you'll be a Man, my son!

In considering what really matters, it is a good idea to reflect on the cherished legacy that our fathers have given each of us. For the most part, it is not an inheritance of money or property, but the thoughts, interests, attitudes, values, and beliefs that have been passed on to us by our fathers. A quotation by Robert Fulgrum states: "Don't worry that children never listen to you. Worry that they are always watching you." What inheritance have you received? What are you passing on to future generations? Is it your best legacy? If not, why not?

Seed of Thought

Law of Success
by Napoleon Hill

MORE SEEDS FOR SUCCESS

by Napoleon Hill

Sow an action and you reap a habit; sow a habit and you reap a character; sow a character and you reap a destiny.

Magic Seed 22

You have within you a sleeping giant who is ready to be awakened and directed by you to the performance of any sort of service you desire. And when you wake up some morning and find yourself on the success beam and in the upper brackets of success, you will wonder why you had not sooner discovered that you had all of the makings of a big success.

–NAPOLEON HILL

Dear Readers:

Summer–it is a time to relax, shift gears, and take some personal time for ourselves. For example, during my high school years summertime was reading and enrichment time. Each grade level was provided a reading list. During this time of iced drinks, cookouts, days at the beach, and evenings on the front porch swing, I and my classmates were supposed to be reading the classics in preparation for the next school year. Looking back, this often seemed like a curse, but now I perceive it as a blessing because my learning did not stop the day school let out in June. Rather, I was introduced to many authors, stories, and cultures that took me on numerous armchair trips that ended in learning new things. Phone calls flew among classmates discussing plot, characterization, setting, and theme. Through these discussions we gained insight from one another as well as the books we read. By the time we finished the last book on the list, our awareness was expanded and we felt as if we had entered the ranks of the next class.

With prices soaring and budgets set, this might not be the summer to take an extensive trip. Why not consider traveling to faraway lands via a book? Emily Dickinson reminds us below that the cost of a book is well worth the investment. Even the poorest of us can acquire a book through purchase, on loan, or via a library card. Why not chart your course for success and prepare yourself for the journey by reading a good book?

There is no frigate like a book
To take us lands away,
Nor any coursers like a page
Of prancing poetry.

This traverse may the poorest take
Without oppress of toll;
How frugal is the chariot
That bears a human soul!

—EMILY DICKINSON

Here are some "classical" and "current" suggestions to get you started on your success course.

1. Napoleon Hill. *Think and Grow Rich*.
2. Napoleon Hill. *Law of Success*.
3. Claude Bristol. *The Magic of Believing*.
4. Dr. Murphy. *The Power of Your Subconscious Mind*.
5. Venice Bloodworth. *Keys to Yourself*.
6. W. Clement Stone. *The Success System that Never Fails*.
7. Napoleon Hill & Judith Williamson. *Poems that Inspire You to Think and Grow Rich*.
8. J. Martin Kohe. *Your Greatest Power*.
9. J. Martin Kohe & Judith Williamson. *How to Become a Mental Millionaire*.
10. Jeffrey Gitomer. *Little Gold Book of Yes! Attitude*.
11. Napoleon Hill and W. Clement Stone. *Success Through a Positive Mental Attitude*.

12. Arnold Fox, M. D. & Barry Fox, Ph.D. ***Beyond Positive Thinking***.
13. Viktor E. Frankl. ***Man's Search for Meaning***.
14. Napoleon Hill & Judith Williamson. ***Timeless Thoughts for Today***.
15. Andrew Bienkowski and Mary Akers. ***Radical Gratitude***.

Looks like the above should keep you busy for the summer months! And, don't forget to share your reading with a friend.

Seed of Thought

Radical Gratitude
by Andrew Bienkowski and Mary Akers

More Seeds for Success

by Napoleon Hill

The creative force of the entire universe functions through your mind when you establish a definite purpose and apply your faith to its fulfillment.

Magic Seed 23

Sometimes it is wiser to join forces with an opponent than it is to fight.
–NAPOLEON HILL

Dear Readers:

Ever heard the expression "you could see it in their eyes"? By making eye contact with a person, we can often sense their intention without hearing a spoken word. Eyes can flash anger, express sympathy, convey romance, and stop a person in their tracks. Eyes have been called the window to the soul, and when you gaze into someone's eyes there can be a sense that you are aligning with their spiritual nature.

Dr. Hill often tells us to make eye contact with ourselves so as to acknowledge the real person in charge of our lives. Rather than placing blame and responsibility on someone or something else for the way our lives have turned out, we need to face up to the person responsible.

Once when dealing with a person seeking his help, Dr. Hill stated: "You came to me for help but I am sorry to tell you that after hearing your story there is not one thing I can do for you. But, I know a man who can help you if he will do it. He is here in this building right now and I will introduce you to him if you wish me to do so." With that, Dr. Hill took the man by the arm and positioned him in front of a long curtain. Next, the curtain was pulled aside and the man saw himself in a full length mirror. Dr. Hill then stated: "There is the man who can help you. He is the only man who can do it, and until you become better acquainted with him and learn to depend upon him you will not find your way out of your present unfortunate condition."

With this plan of action and the prop of the mirror, Dr. Hill made a very significant impression on the man seeking his help. Realizing that all his complaints, trials and tribulations, and mounting bad luck were of his own making, the man thanked Dr. Hill for not coddling him and went off and turned his life around.

The moral of this story is obvious. We are each given one life at birth to live to the fullest extent regardless of the difficulties we encounter. Our glass of life can be viewed either half full or half empty. If life becomes meaningless, it is because we have not given our lives meaning. Sometimes a little shock treatment such as the above mirror technique will jar us back into reality and help us focus. The life we live is the life we co-create for ourselves. If it is not to our liking, then we need to correct our vision and see by seeing with more passionate eyes. Otherwise, we could be blinded to our true and everlasting self.

Ella Wheeler Wilcox was a contemporary of Dr. Hill. He often quoted from her poems in his works. The poem entitled *"Attainment"* which is reprinted below carries on the visioning theme. Read and reflect, and then consider how you can advance yourself by focusing on your life's vision, attainment, and destiny.

ATTAINMENT

by Ella Wheeler Wilcox

Use all your hidden forces. Do not miss
The purpose of this life, and do not wait
For circumstance to mould or change your fate.
In your own self lies Destiny. Let this
Vast truth cast out all fear, all prejudice,
All hesitation. Know that you are great,
Great with divinity. So dominate
Environment, and enter into bliss.
Love largely and hate nothing. Hold no aim
That does not chord with universal good.

Hear what the voices of the Silence say,
All joys are yours if you put forth your claim.
Once let the spiritual laws be understood,
Material things must answer and obey.

Seed of Thought

Poems of Ella Wheeler Wilcox
by Ella Wheeler Wilcox

More Seeds for Success

by Napoleon Hill

Count the day lost if the setting sun finds you with no good deeds done.

Magic Seed 24

Concentration is the ability, through fixed habit and practice, to keep your mind on one subject until you have thoroughly familiarized yourself with that subject and mastered it.

–NAPOLEON HILL

Dear Readers:

W. Clement Stone states: "Remember, we will fail our heritage only when we no longer try." This statement is worth considering. As I read it, I wonder what Stone meant by the word ***try***. Try can be an ambiguous word. It can represent many things. In ***The Empire Strikes Back***, Yoda states: "Do or do not. There is no try." Stone's most famous command is "Do it now!" So, what does he mean when he challenges us to try?

Perhaps trying precedes doing. Trying could be the incubation period that is essential before the doing part can happen. July 4th is a good time to remember what our forefathers contributed to our freedom. Without them, where would we be? As we try to imagine life without the freedoms we enjoy, it may just encourage us to not only remember but to act. When the time comes to preserve freedom for ourselves and others, we can then recall why we do so and act accordingly.

We know that thought precedes action. Dr. Hill reminds us that "what we think about we become." As we think about freedom, perhaps it is good to think back and try to remember what there is to enjoy about it. Thinking back can be an important time to reflect on those individuals who enabled us to live freely today. By remembering their personal sacrifices to secure our freedom, we might be inspired to do the same if and when the time comes.

Truly courageous acts are those done in the spirit of service and regard for others. Working in a soup kitchen, assisting the elderly, playing with children in need of human contact, enabling people to become independent through employment, and serving our country through the Armed Forces, are all ways to give testimony to the personal freedoms we enjoy today. Simply by lending a helping hand, we are endorsing the fact that we are free to do so.

It becomes our opportunity to learn about historical events that brought us to where we are today, and next carry the positive message we extract from these events into the future. This July 4th, let's remember why we are grateful and celebrate all that is good and beneficial about our country. Begin this July 4th to reflect on our history and next imagine what good we can do in the future to not only continue the legacy but to improve upon it for all societies of the world to enjoy now and forever.

Seed of Thought

Napoleon Hill's Positive Action Plan: 365 Meditations for Making Each Day a Success
by Napoleon Hill

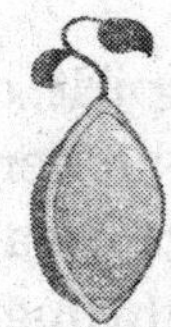

Magic Seed 25

The richest copper mine in the world was discovered by a miner who had spent most of his life searching for gold. His trusty mule, which carried all of his worldly belongings, including his mining equipment, fell into a gopher hole, broke his leg and had to be shot. While trying to dig the mule's leg out of the hole, the rich copper ore was uncovered.

–NAPOLEON HILL

Dear Readers:

In everyone's life some rain must fall. When we are in the midst of experiencing what some have called the "dark night of the soul" it may appear that the sun has set for eternity. Pulling ourselves up by our bootstraps becomes too much of an effort, and seeing the good in the bad sounds like insanity. Still, when we begin to sense there is a glimmer of hope–maybe only the tiny light emitted by a firefly on a summer's night–we begin to believe that we might be able to overcome this adversity glowworm by glowworm, inch by inch.

Remember the myth about Pandora? When the box full of evils was released on the world, something tiny and radiant remained in the very bottom of the chest. It crept out slowly, and was called Hope! Hope may be the smallest treasure in the box, but we all know that size does not determine value. The Hope diamond is smaller than many mansions around the world, but holds significantly greater worth. Hope replaces the emptiness that adversity leaves behind. Hope can expand to equal and then exceed the adversity that it replaces–if only we believe.

Belief can make it so. Dr. Hill states: "What the mind can conceive and believe, the mind can achieve." If we believe in Hope, it will arrive on fairy wings and begin the process of enabling us to overcome our adversities. Light and airy does not mean silly and stupid, but rather something that is tender and in need of nurturing.

Cherish hope the way you worry about adversity and soon hope will illuminate your attitude and drive away adversity's darkness. It is a proven fact that our minds cannot hold two simultaneous thoughts at once. Why not cultivate thoughts of hope, and plant the seeds of success where weeds once grew? Your mind is the garden, you are the gardener, and you select the crop. Which will you choose? In the end, you must decide.

In closing, consider the poem entitled *Life* by Ella Wheeler Wilcox, and ask yourself how you can move out of darkness into the light. Remember, "Don't take away someone's hope. It may be all that they have left."

LIFE

by Ella Wheeler Wilcox

All in the dark we grope along,
And if we go amiss
We learn at least which path is wrong,
And there is gain in this.

We do not always win the race
By only running right,
We have to tread the mountain's base
Before we reach its height.

But he who loves himself the last
And knows the use of pain,
Though strewn with errors all his past,
He surely shall attain.

Some souls there are that needs must taste
Of wrong, ere choosing right;
We should not call those years a waste
Which led us to the light.

Seed of Thought

The Power of Believing by Claude Bristol

Magic Seed 26

Remember that those things that have never been done before offer the greatest challenge and opportunity. The pioneer who first accomplishes them is the one who reaps the reward.

–NAPOLEON HILL

Dear Readers:

Dr. Hill often credits what the maintenance of a positive mental attitude can do for your outlook on life as well as your success. You are your greatest asset. And, who are you? Why, you are a combination of your past life experiences and current thoughts. Even if your past is not how you envision your future, you can always begin anew to chart your journey to success.

Whether we like it or not, our thoughts create our outcomes. Generous people think generous thoughts. Selfish people think selfish thoughts. A generous person cannot turn into a selfish one without changing the basis of his or her thoughts and vice versa. But, you may ask, how does one condition one's mind for a positive mental attitude? Sometimes it's not easy, but it can always be accomplished if the person is aware that thoughts are the foundational building blocks of action.

Napoleon Hill says it best when he states that "Thoughts are things." At first, this statement may even make one laugh because it sounds ludicrous. But, thinking more in depth, one begins to realize that thoughts are really "things" that do create tangible outcomes. We often hear this about words too. Words are a vocalization of thought and do impact the world. Campaigns are run on words, friendships are built on words, words precede love, and love creates our world. Just think about it for a few minutes, and you will concur that thoughts are truly things and each of us empowers our thoughts to create the physical reality of our world one actualized idea at a time. If thoughts can and do formulate into the words that we speak, is it any wonder then that thoughts expressed in words can shape our day by day reality? Thought transformed into things is truly a marvel of our human potential at its greatest.

Sister Deborah, a member of the Poor Handmaids of Jesus Christ, has transformed her thoughts of service into a program that directly relates to putting food on the table for 25 indigenous women in Mexico. The program that she has created out of her thoughts now enables these women to do work that not only enhances their self-esteem, but also contributes to the livelihood of their families directly. Whether it is the money that they earn, or the food that they bring home, Sister Deborah's program is making a difference for these women in a very respectable, entrepreneurial way. "What the mind can conceive and believe, the mind can achieve" is a famous quotation coined by Dr. Hill and put into immediate practice in the program in Mexico. Sister Deborah is overcoming one limitation at a time by doing her very best to give meaningful employment to all the women that her ministry touches. I will conclude as she signs off in her emails, "Be well. God bless you REAL good." That's thought at its best!

Seed of Thought

Key to Yourself
by Venice Bloodworth

Magic Seed 27

Patience demands its own peculiar kind of courage. It's a persistent type of forbearance and fortitude that results from complete dedication to an ideal or goal. Therefore, the more strongly you are imbued with the idea of achieving your principal goal in life, the more patience you will have to overcome obstacles.

–NAPOLEON HILL

Dear Readers:

It's true. Our lives seem to be the busiest ever, and our minds follow the pattern of our lives. Just "being" becomes more and more difficult as each day begins with more to do and the chatter in our minds becomes non-stop. How do we become still and learn to listen to the innate wisdom inside each of us? How can we learn to turn down the constant noise, and tune in to that still small voice within that knows us intimately?

When we are able to disengage ourselves from the constant mind chatter, we find that not only do we gain more time, but we can effectively channel into our personal genius and become creatively inspired. That's good for us and good for our soul too. When this occurs, time slows down, stress lessens, we are alert to our surroundings in the now, and do not project ourselves into the future, or time travel to the past, but stay constructively engaged in the present–the only real time there is.

In the times when I am able to stay constructively in the present, I am more centered, less stressed. I complete tasks effortlessly, and still have time remaining. I enjoy the moment and feel part of the eternal now. Days like this are calming, constructive, creative, and centering. I feel as if I could engage in any task and have a successful outcome. I will be the first to admit that these days are not typical, but I would like more of them. As I seek the recipe for this type of day, I notice some commonalities in their overall structure.

First, I disengage myself from the outcome. I do my best and then forget about it. I do not fret, cajole, mourn, or grieve for what is or isn't. I accept just "is." Second, I move from task to task with a direct approach, but not a compulsion. I greet it, complete it, and walk away from it allowing the universe to deal with its outcome instead of me. Third, I attend to my inner and outer world. What's physical aligns with spirit, and vice versa. This creates equilibrium. And, balance is good. Fourth, I look for the humor in the situation, rather than look for something to critique. Humor tickles our spirit, and criticism slaps it down. Finally, I follow the flow, and do not attempt to change the course of the river. For me, days like this are memorable and speak to my spirit. And it is on a day like this that I am open to miracles small and large. Insights come and go, synchronicities happen, and positive results are tangible.

I read a reflection this morning that took me on a reverie because I like ships, sailing, and anything to do with water. Written by Terry Lynn Taylor and Mary Beth Crain it states: "My life is floating in a sea of tranquility; my body is the boat, my mind the sail, and my soul the water." If this doesn't calm you down and help you practice patience, I can't imagine what will! As you sail away on life's oceans, may all your journeys be filled with positive destinations.

Seed of Thought

Napoleon Hill's First Editions
by Napoleon Hill

Magic Seed 28

I refuse to believe what you say unless it harmonizes with what you do.
—NAPOLEON HILL

Dear Readers:

I do not know if you have heard of Charlie "T" Jones or read his book *Life is Tremendous*, but if not you need to get on the success beam and order one right away. Charlie's life, lectures, and his many publications have profoundly influenced those lucky enough to have crossed his path. Charlie's focus never waivers. When I phoned him last week to thank him for positive comments that he made on something I had written, the focus of the phone call was not on Charlie's health, but on how much he enjoyed what I had written.

This simple phone call encapsulated for me the life of a man who made his work his ministry. Known for his big bear hugs, Charlie will run through the pearly gates embracing God in the biggest hug ever when his time comes. How do I know this? I know it because I have been the recipient of Charlie's big hugs and even God could not refuse one from him accompanied with the unconditional love he offers. Charlie changes lives by hugs! Even now, I can feel the warmth of his hug and his accompanying positive messages.

Napoleon Hill states: "No man can be truly happy until he translates the words of the Golden Rule into deeds, and shares happiness with others." Charlie is a living example of this mandate for success. Humor is the vehicle for Charlie's Christian message. After attending a breakfast talk a few years ago, my husband stated that Charlie was the best speaker that he ever heard. Not only did he believe it, but he echoed the sentiment of well over 400 people in the audience. It was a packed house and there was not a dry eye due to so much laughing. Yes, humor and hugs are two of Charlie's trademarks.

Charlie's third trademark is his honesty. His hugs and humor all enable him to touch someone's spirit. And when he has opened the door of a person's spiritual side, he is able to sneak in and give honest, personalized advice that hits home every time because it does not involve criticism but rather praise. Charlie has the unique ability of causing a person to look within themselves and reflect upon what they can give to others.

Finally, Charlie's fourth trademark is home. I have visited his house on two occasions and both times I have left astounded as to the gifts that he gives to his hometown community. Charlie has a Christmas room set up year round that entertains young people that are in need of a little tender loving care. He has several libraries, one in particular being a library of books that are biographical. He loves reading biographies because they teach him lessons that he can use in his own life. When he speaks in person, he persuades people to read by passionately kissing books. This is a remarkable image because the audience begins to wonder what is so special about the books that he kisses. He arouses their interest enough to send them running to the bookstore to buy whatever book is being kissed this week.

So hugs, humor, honesty and home are what Charlie delivers to anyone and everyone who crosses his path. I will conclude with this prayer by St. Thomas More.

> *Give me, Lord, a soul that knows nothing of boredom, groans and sighs. Never let me be overly concerned for this inconstant thing I call me. Lord, give me a sense of humor so that I may take some happiness from this life and share it with others.*

I am convinced that when this prayer was heard, God created Charlie! And, we are all thankful for the wonderful gifts that Charlie has given to all of us who know him already and those of you who will meet him in his wonderful, motivational book ***Life Is Tremendous***.

P. S. Charlie "T" Jones had his Homecoming on October 16, 2008. He returned home on Boss' Day. Last I heard, he was still giving those big bear hugs to all who crossed the threshold before he did.

Seed of Thought

Life is Tremendous
by Charlie "T" Jones

More Seeds for Success

by Napoleon Hill

The orderliness of the world of natural laws gives evidence that they are under the control of a universal plan.

Magic Seed 29

The necessity for struggle is one of the unique ways that the Creator has provided to force people to develop and expand their mind-powers and gain wisdom. Wherever that necessity is removed the individual becomes soft and lacking in the resourcefulness with which to avail himself of his worldly needs.

–NAPOLEON HILL

Dear Readers:

Andrew Carnegie states: "There is no use whatever trying to help people who do not help themselves. You cannot push anyone up a ladder unless he is willing to climb himself." Before a person can practice the art of persistence, the will to achieve must be firmly planted in both the subconscious and conscious minds. You probably have heard the quote, "Where there's a will, there's a way." Actually the reverse applies also, "No will, no way!" Our ongoing self-talk over time creates habit patterns that become self-fulfilling prophecies. When we consider this, it is apparent that what we think about we become, therefore, if we think about succeeding in life persistence will enable us to accomplish our goal sooner or later.

Albert Einstein states: "I think and think for months and years. Ninety-nine times, the conclusion is false. The hundredth time I am right." This is persistence in action. Thought is an action. Being an active "doer" enables us to call into effect the Law of Averages. It's a known fact that over time things gravitate to the middle, just by doing something repeatedly insures that we will get some consistent result over time. By directing our thoughts toward what it is we want, and then taking action on those thoughts we are activating the Law of Averages. Why else would we try and try again if at first we don't succeed? Simply because we are hopeful that the tide will change, the cycle will be on the upswing, the market will be bullish, and we will experience success due to our hard work.

When asked if he walked on water, legendary Alabama football coach Bear Bryant states: "Well, I won't say I can or I can't; but if I do, I do it before most people get up in the morning." One key to success is imbedded in the quote above and it is self-discipline. Just as Coach Bryant implies, nothing much will happen without self-discipline—persistence will not, personal initiative will not, budgeting time and money will not, going the extra mile will not. You've heard it stated too that "good things come to those who wait" and while those people are waiting I can imagine that they are persistently doing things that will place them on the road to success.

One last quote—and it's a favorite of mine. Emerson states: "Do the thing and you shall have the power." I imagine that Emerson's emphasis is on the word **DO** and not power since this is a command. The operative word is do and do is an action word. Following the directive, if you do continually, you are persistent, and those who persist usually end up being the winners they knew they were all along.

Seed of Thought

Collected Works of Ralph Waldo Emerson
by Ralph Waldo Emerson

Magic Seed 30

Any person who attains a high degree of success usually starts off by putting everything they have behind a single objective. They stay on a single track until they get to their destination. After that, they may branch out by setting new goals for themselves.

—NAPOLEON HILL

Dear Readers:

As much as we may dislike it, it pays to concentrate. Why? Because when we concentrate we do not scatter our energies. This one principle can make us more efficient and prepare us for the "big" break that may be just around the corner. Andrew Carnegie states: "Controlled attention is the act of combining all the forces of the mind and fixing them upon the attainment of a definite purpose." Carnegie focused upon the manufacturing and marketing of steel. His interest was not a passing fancy, rather an obsession. Because of the magnitude of his obsession, his concentration diminished the competition. His controlled attention prepared him for opportunities that the average person would not even have recognized. Chance meeting preparedness is one definition of the word luck. In this regard, Carnegie was definitely a very lucky person.

With Carnegie's story in mind, how then can we enhance our success opportunities through concentration? Dr. Hill explains that over a period of time thought that is emotionalized imprints upon the subconscious mind and works to a person's advantage even while the person sleeps. Over time practical plans for the attainment of our desire are created in the subconscious mind and then "flashed" into the conscious mind at unexpected moments. Our job is to be ready to receive the plan and to act on it at once. These insights are distilled thoughts that have been processed to our best advantage by our higher thinking source–the subconscious mind. Whether you call it inspiration, that "still, small voice within," a message from beyond, or a hunch, you need to recognize it for what it is, the opportunity in the form of a plan to attain your greatest desire.

Enthusiasm is a by-product of concentration. While in the "flow" of controlled attention, enthusiasm enters the process and functions as the accelerant that adds the fuel to enable us to make it to the finish line. Minor tasks, done with controlled attention, take on an enthusiasm of their own. Entering the process with a positive mental attitude creates the proper atmosphere for these tasks to be accomplished. Drudgery occurs when we do not hold a positive mental attitude while actually doing the work. Be alert, be confident, be directed, and be industrious. These traits combined with a positive mental attitude are the ingredients of a winner.

As you learn to control the tasks placed in front of you, eventually you will learn to take complete control of your mind. One of my favorite quotes on this subject is by Harriet Beecher Stowe. It reads: "When you get into a tight place and everything goes against you, 'til it seems as though you could not hold on a minute longer, never give up then, for that is just the place and time that the tide will turn." Know that when the tide turns in your favor you will have mastered the art of controlled attention and used it to your greater purpose.

Seed of Thought

Think and Grow Rich Action Pack
by Napoleon Hill

Magic Seed 31

A positive mental attitude brings with it faith, enthusiasm, personal initiative, self-discipline, imagination and definiteness of purpose which attract people and beneficial opportunities.

–NAPOLEON HILL

Dear Readers:

Having and maintaining a positive mental attitude should be first on your daily list of items to accomplish just like taking a bath and brushing your teeth. It's more important than taking out the garbage, giving the cat a bath, preparing a gourmet dinner, or paying your bills. Sounds unreasonable, doesn't it? Not really, because without a Positive Mental Attitude the items on your to-do list won't matter anyway. Unless you predispose your life for success, it won't happen spontaneously. Conditioning your mind for PMA is like watching for a shooting star, expecting to see a rainbow after a storm, anticipating the rose inside of the bud, counting the days until your new kitten purrs, and deciding on dessert before you finish your main course. There is nothing wrong and everything right with setting your mind on a course of positive action. It's the expectation that makes the event extra-special, not only the event itself. As you color your world the way you desire it, more often than not you are stepping into the future one positive thought at a time.

What are some simple ways that you can secure a positive outcome for yourself on a daily basis? Perhaps the list below can give you some ideas that can be put into practice.

1. Get a head start by affirming to your subconscious

mind before you fall asleep that when you awake it will be a fantastic day! Create a little rhyme like: "When I awake it will be great!" Repeat it as you fall asleep.

2. Before getting up stretch and linger as you become conscious. When fully awake, remind yourself that today will be just spectacular.
3. Take a few minutes for quiet time before you jumpstart your routine. Have a lingering cup of coffee, witness what is occurring out-of-doors, watch the birds at the feeder, and then express a prayer of gratitude for all you have been given today and every day.
4. Make time to list in writing what you intend to accomplish this day. Keep your primary to-do list reasonable and under five items. Have some easy, medium, and hard things to accomplish this day. Challenge yourself to move through your list and complete the items one by one.
5. Be less serious. Allow humor to enter your life. Laugh and laugh again. A good laugh is like a massage for the soul.
6. Give up perfection and be satisfied with good enough on things that are really not that important. Polishing the silver is good for the family heirloom, but is it making a profound difference in your life?
7. Focus daily on something that makes your heart expand not contract. If you are not living for something spectacular, then why are you living for less?
8. Extend yourself daily by doing a kindness for another that is not meant to be reciprocated. Do it and forget it!
9. Elevate your spiritual nature by reading a section of a classical book. Better yet, make a list of 12 classics that you decide to read this year. Challenge yourself to one good book a month.
10. Remember to pay it forward! Stockpile your harvest for your future needs. Do not let the well run dry for lack of priming the pump! Give before you get!

These little techniques may not make you an overnight success, but they will set your feet in motion toward a better life.

Seed of Thought

The Power of Positive Thinking
by Norman Vincent Peale

More Seeds for Success

by Napoleon Hill

You, too, can ride the success beam by learning to discover and build on the seed of an equivalent benefit in each of your setbacks.

Magic Seed 32

The successful person has a keen respect for his Creator and expresses it frequently through prayers and deeds of helpfulness to others. The failure believes in nothing but his own desire for food and shelter, and seeks these at the expense of others when and where he can.

–NAPOLEON HILL

Dear Readers:

Have you ever wondered why some people have a phenomenal success rate and others can barely make the grade? Why is it that those who succeed more often than not continue to experience ongoing success and those who fail also repeat the pattern of failure? Dr. Hill enlightens us as to why this happens. He removes the mystery and cuts to the chase by using a comparison/contrast method. His examples juxtapose the actions of the successful person with the actions of the person who fails. When placed side by side it is easy to see what makes the ultimate difference between a success and a failure.

Here are some of the characteristics of those who succeed. Upon reviewing these personality traits, ask yourself which ones you possess. If you would like to increase your rate of success, work on the ones you lack. You will see a remarkable difference in your success rate in a very short period of time when you focus on changing your behavior to match the behavior of those who succeed.

1. The successful person has a plan for getting what he wants, has faith in his ability to acquire it, and works his plan.
2. The successful person is obliging and friendly. He encourages others through his positive mental attitude

to assist him in achieving his goals.

3. The successful person is tactful. He thinks before he speaks and anticipates the reaction of his audience as he engages their cooperation.
4. The successful person keeps his opinions to himself for the most part, and only expresses those that he has researched and can be backed by facts.
5. The successful person budgets his time and money wisely.
6. The successful person is genuinely interested in all people.
7. The successful person is open-minded and tolerant of others.
8. The successful person remains current and knows what is occurring locally, nationally, and internationally.
9. The successful person focuses on the positive and eliminates the negative.
10. The successful person is a giver first and a receiver second. His primary focus is on the service he renders.
11. The successful person respects the Creator and acknowledges Him for all the gifts he has been given and is yet to receive.

The above traits of successful people can be descriptive of you too! First, however, make certain that you truly do model these characteristics–not just imagine that you do. After each of the specifics list the actions that you have taken to ground these points in reality not just thought. Remember–Thought + Action = SUCCESS. Certainly, what you think about you become, as long as your thinking inspires the correct action that you take in manifesting the behavior. Just as Michelangelo saw David in the block of stone he sculpted, so too can you see the person you will become as you apply these success traits in sculpting your success personality.

Seed of Thought

Succeed and Grow Rich Through Persuasion
by Napoleon Hill

Magic Seed 33

Flexibility is the one trait that softens poverty and adorns riches for it helps you to be grateful for your blessings and unabashed by misfortune. It can help you, too, to make beneficial use of every experience of life, whether pleasant or unpleasant.

–NAPOLEON HILL

Dear Readers:

Flexibility enhances your effectiveness in many ways. It does not mean giving up your own viewpoints, but rather being open enough to hear and consider the views of another. By being flexible in your interactions with others you add to your knowledge base and this paves the way for the ongoing development of your own pleasing personality. In this manner working relationships can be established that promote harmony in understanding the ideas, attitudes, and customs of another. This type of experiential learning gives everyone the opportunity to "taste test" another's world view. If you find it to your liking, you can adopt it for your own. Perhaps it may require more than one exposure for you to develop a taste for the new idea, attitude, or custom. Added exposure may help determine whether or not you want to assimilate this new thing into your life. Remember, you can always select it or decline it. The choice is yours.

Think back to the first time you were offered a new food that you had not experienced before. When you first tasted it, you may have liked it instantly if it were similar to something you already enjoyed. But, if the food were something that you had never tasted, you had no immediate basis of comparison. In that instance, you had one of three reactions: like, dislike, or neutrality. The "neutral" reception left you open to experience the item again with the possibility of making a choice of next eating it or avoiding it. Either way, you learned a lesson, and that lesson would have been unavailable to you if you never accepted the challenge of trying something new.

I remember a time when I avoided mangos because my first impression of them was distasteful. Years later, my niece encouraged me to try some in Arizona that she had peeled and prepared for a simple luncheon. When I tried them, they were ripe and delicious, unlike my previous experience. Although I still do not like peeling mangos, I enjoy eating them when ripe varieties are available. So, through flexibility, my thinking and experiences changed.

Napoleon Hill states that: "One who is lacking in flexibility of mind is not qualified for leadership in business or industry, or for any kind of supervisory position where success depends upon the cooperation of others." Relating to only those employees who are like you can alienate the remainder of the workforce. Relating to everyone based on their personality instills the cooperative effort that creates success. People come in many packages, and in order to create harmony and cooperation, it's best to be open and amenable to experiencing the best that each individual has to offer. Why not try something new? Connect with someone who is not just like you. See what develops, and watch the growth of your own personality as you adopt a new idea, attitude, or custom because of this connection.

Seed of Thought

Beyond Positive Thinking
by Arnold Fox, M.D. & Barry Fox, Ph. D

Magic Seed 34

No one is "born enthusiastic." It is a trait that is acquired. You can acquire it, too. Remember that in almost every contact with others you are trying, in a sense, to sell them something. That's true in all except trivial relationships. First convince yourself of the value of your idea, your product, your service–or yourself. Examine it—or yourself—critically. Learn the flaws in whatever you are trying to sell—and eliminate or correct them. Be thoroughly convinced of the "rightness" of your product or idea.

–NAPOLEON HILL

Dear Readers:

Enthusiasm is a powerful motivator when it is sincere and heartfelt. It is a spirit that inspires us to move forward positively in a direction of our own choosing. It lightens our daily burdens, puts a spring in our step, a genuine smile on our face, and as the old saying goes "a song in our heart." Only the results of enthusiasm can be seen, not enthusiasm itself because it is an abstract concept. Love, faith, honor, loyalty, and beauty are also abstract concepts. They cannot be perceived directly with the naked eye, but can be seen indirectly in the results that they cause to happen.

When one is enthusiastic, burdens become lighter, worry takes a step back, and faith moves to the forefront. A "can-do attitude" accompanies enthusiasm and erases any lingering negativity. People feel that an enthusiastic person can overcome great obstacles because it appears that the entire universe is conspiring to bring about the desire that the person has set their heart on acquiring. A certain charisma develops within the enthusiastic person. Crowds respond to the "electricity" that this person generates when they walk into a room, address a crowd, deliver a speech, or just work for their cause. Enthusiasm becomes a catalyst for change when it is sincere. People jump on the bandwagon of an enthusiastic person because they want to feel the energy for themselves. Greatness demands enthusiasm. A milquetoast personality is never described as enthusiastic.

To be enthusiastic, act enthusiastically. Allow yourself to feel the energy and lightness of being that develops when you embrace the higher vibrations of your spirit. It's said that angels can fly because they take themselves lightly. We also can learn to fly by being more enthusiastic. The more spirit filled we are, the less bound to the mundane we become. To be enthusiastic, embrace the spirit within. Next, allow that spirit to bring you to new heights of achievement. You will be soaring before you even realize that your feet have left the ground!

In conclusion, I would like to share a poem by Ella Wheeler Wilcox. Although she does not specifically mention enthusiasm, her poem tells us how to use our higher powers involving thoughts and outcomes. Our thoughts shape our lives, and consequently affect the lives of those around us too. Think good thoughts—preordain good outcomes. This idea alone is worthy of our enthusiastic response.

WISHING

by Ella Wheeler Wilcox

Do you wish the world were better?
Let me tell you what to do.
Set a watch upon your actions,
Keep them always straight and true.
Rid your mind of selfish motives,
Let your thoughts be clean and high.
You can make a little Eden
Of the sphere you occupy.

Do you wish the world were wiser?
Well, suppose you make a start,
By accumulating wisdom
In the scrapbook of your heart;
Do not waste one page on folly;
Live to learn, and learn to live.
If you want to give men knowledge
You must get it, ere you give.

Do you wish the world were happy?
Then remember day by day
Just to scatter seeds of kindness
As you pass along the way,
For the pleasures of the many
May be ofttimes traced to one,
As the hand that plants an acorn
Shelters armies from the sun.

Seed of Thought

The Master-Key to Riches
by Napoleon Hill

MORE SEEDS FOR SUCCESS

by Napoleon Hill

Render more and better service than that for which you are paid and sooner or later you'll receive compound interest on compound interest from your investment. It is inevitable that every seed of service you sow will multiply and come back to you in overwhelming abundance.

Magic Seed 35

Is it possible that you have imprisoned your mind in a social and cultural concentration camp? Have you subjected yourself to a brain-washing of your own making, isolating you from ideas that could lead to success? If so, it's time to sweep aside the bars of prejudice that imprison your intellect.

–NAPOLEON HILL

Dear Readers:

Have you allowed yourself to become stagnant, old, and self-centered before your time? Have eccentricities and hardening of your attitudes prevented you from experiencing anything new? Do you find yourself saying "no" more than "yes"? Well, if these are your symptoms then your diagnosis is an early demise from a productive life! A person's ability to change is tantamount to his or her ability to grow and expand in life's overabundant awareness. Rigidity, or lack of the ability to change, is only a spiral downward to death and dying. Which end of the spiral do you prefer to be on? Yes, it is true. When you're green you grow. When you're ripe you rot. Not a very pleasant thought, is it?

Changing our habits of attitudes that have cemented themselves into the patterns of our life may require a jackhammer, but it is worth it. By telling yourself "no" to the mundane, ordinary, and commonplace, you alert your spirit to the changes you are about to embrace. Next time, when presented with an opportunity to move out of your comfort zone, accept it with glee instead of with a sigh. Be enthusiastic as a newborn is enthusiastic about exploring the world. Look with new eyes and be encouraged or "given a new heart" when it comes to trying new things.

Begin simply. If someone suggests a new restaurant for lunch, do not respond with "I don't eat that type of food," but say instead, "I will give it a try." When shopping for clothes, don't always visit the same store and department that you have purchased from for decades, but rather explore something that might make you feel youthful, more colorful, or even more alluring. If invited to visit a place such as a museum, art show, book store, carnival, opera, musical, or whatever that normally does not excite you, decide that it is the Universe sending you an opportunity to do something new.

Once when I was asked to submit a proposal for a session to the American Society for Quality's annual world conference in Seattle, I almost declined because I thought that our interests were dissimilar. Well, now having presented at the World Conference, an affiliate conference in Australia, and a local chapter in Tennessee, I am glad that I did not decline the opportunity to submit a proposal to ASQ because of my own reservations. Sometimes, the Universe provides us opportunities for growth right on schedule. Do not fail to return the RSVP from the Universe. You might just be missing the very best thing life has to offer at this moment. See you there!

Seed of Thought

Man's Search for Ultimate Meaning
by Viktor E. Frankl

Magic Seed 36

Without humility you will never be able to find what I call the "seed of equivalent benefit" in adversity and defeat. Every adversity or defeat, I have found, carries with it something to help you overcome it—and even rise above it.

—NAPOLEON HILL

Dear Readers:

Napoleon Hill states that man's greatest advances have been based on true humility. It does not matter whether these advances are spiritual, cultural, or material because true humility knows no bounds. Humility assists man for his own good and the good of others. It is a trait that seeks no recognition, recoils from publicity, and removes the self from the equation. It puts the service project first for the definite major purpose of the betterment of mankind and worries about the practicalities later. Humble people are doers who work for the good of the whole and refuse to become encumbered with traditional procedures and technicalities. "To make the world a better place in which to live" is the enduring mantra of the humble person who seeks improvement for all, not just self.

How does one recognize a humble person with these gifts? St. Francis of Assisi has outlined the traits in a popular prayer. He notes that peace, love, pardon, faith, hope, light, and joy are all ways of approaching and finding humility. Usually, a humble person has gone through personal adversity and has come to realize that in himself he is not "all that."

When the light bulb goes off and one realizes that what is done to another is also done to self, one's intent and focus change dramatically. The trait is actualized when true humility begins to foster actions that are performed for others rather than self. When the concept of service blended with gratitude enter the equation, a person's pleasing personality knows no boundaries. Recall the truly humble personalities throughout history who have contributed to the betterment of mankind because they were the opposite of war, hatred, injury, doubt, despair, darkness, and sadness. Not only have they achieved greatness because they have surpassed self, but they have bestowed greatness upon others with their gift of service beyond recognition.

Consider the prayer of St. Francis of Assisi quoted below and how it relates to Dr. Hill's definition of humility. It is a good one to memorize and use as both auto-suggestion and a self-starter toward making this world a better place in which to live–today and every day!

Prayer of St. Francis of Assisi

Lord, make me an instrument of Your peace.
Where there is hatred, let me sow love;
Where there is injury, pardon;
Where there is doubt, faith;
Where there is despair, hope;
Where there is darkness, light;
And where there is sadness, joy.

O Divine Master,
Grant that I may not so much seek
To be consoled as to console;
To be understood as to understand;
To be loved as to love;
For it is in giving that we receive;
It is in pardoning that we are pardoned;
And it is in dying that we are born to eternal life.

Seed of Thought

Timeless Thoughts for Today
by Napoleon Hill and Judith Williamson

Magic Seed 37

Then learn to use the right word in the right place at the right time. This comes only from practice in everyday conversation. As of this moment, erase completely from your vocabulary all profanity, blasphemy, obscenity, or irreverence. The use of profanity or blasphemy is a dead giveaway that one lacks the word-power to express his emotions properly. Obscenity, off-color jokes and the double entendre are resorted to only by the boor who lacks the cleverness to be really funny or amusing. Irreverence, to one's own Deity or that of others, is always in unforgivably bad taste.

–NAPOLEON HILL

Dear Readers:

Sticks and stones can break my bones, but words can never hurt me. I am sure you have heard this saying before and may have even recited it yourself. But how true is it? Name calling, taunting, teasing, verbal abuse, sarcasm and more all solicit a negative response when we permit it to happen. Still, many people believe that there is little power in the spoken word because it is not tangible. How untrue that is. The immediate and direct outcomes of words are always observable and measurable. Just chastise a child, criticize an employee, curse a spouse, or condemn a co-worker and watch what happens. People either shrivel up or attack when an onslaught of verbal abuse confronts them. Seldom do they remain neutral. Even if the reaction is only visible on the inside, the result is instantaneous. Words can be spirit breakers or spirit igniters.

Words, as Napoleon Hill reminds us, should be selected

with precision. They should be used consciously to propel us forward to success, not position us on the brink of disaster. Words can create worlds yet unseen through the creative use of the imagination. Dr. Hill's most famous quotation, "What the mind can conceive and believe, the mind can achieve," tells us explicitly that the thought is the thing that begins its manifestation process via words. Thoughts and words all precede the actions that create the results of our initial thinking.

It's interesting to note that magicians always have "magic words" or "magic formulas" that are spoken before the results are revealed. These magical words condition our minds for what is to follow. We anticipate a rabbit being pulled out of the hat, and that is what we see. We expect flowers to materialize from inside the silk scarf, and that is exactly what happens. Our goals manifest in the same exact way. It can be said that seeing is believing, but it can be stated that believing is seeing as well. Must you see your outcome before your believe it, or can you envision it in your mind's eye before projecting your vision into reality? When we envision prior to physically seeing, we create our future one frame at a time. When we wait to actually see what the future holds for us, we are allowing outside forces to control our results. Better to use positive words to form our mental images that when strongly held and emotionalized create our chosen outcomes. As we begin to understand how the mind works and how things manifest over time, we can begin to control our destiny one positive word at a time.

Below is a poem that Napoleon Hill read. The author, Ella Wheeler Wilcox, was a student of the mind, and her keen insights on the nature of the thought process are well worth remembering. She reminds us poetically that whatever thoughts go out from our mind always come back around to help or hurt us. So, be careful of the words you use and the thoughts you think.

YOU NEVER CAN TELL

by Ella Wheeler Wilcox

You never can tell when you send a word,
Like an arrow shot from a bow
By an archer blind, be it cruel or kind,
Just where it may chance to go.
It may pierce the breast of your dearest friend.
Tipped with its poison or balm,
To a stranger's heart in life's great mart,
It may carry its pain or its calm.

You never can tell when you do an act
Just what the result will be;
But with every deed you are sowing a seed,
Through the harvest you may not see.
Each kindly act is an acorn dropped
In God's productive soil.
You may not know, but the tree shall grow,
With shelter for those who toil.

You never can tell what your thoughts will do,
In bringing you hate or love;
For thoughts are things, and their airy wings
Are swifter than carrier doves.
They follow the law of the universe–
Each thing must create its kind,
And they speed o'er the track to bring you back
Whatever went out from your mind.

Seed of Thought

Your Word Is Your Wand
by Florence Scovel Shinn

More Seeds for Success

by Napoleon Hill

Remember to express gratitude every day—by prayer and affirmation—for the blessings you already have.

Magic Seed 38

Rightly or wrongly, human nature is such that first impressions usually are the ones that endure. More important, the first impression may be the only one we have a chance to make. Therefore, it must be good!

–NAPOLEON HILL

Dear Readers:

Napoleon Hill Yesterday and Today is the inspirational ezine published by the Napoleon Hill Foundation. Whether you are a new subscriber or a charter member, I believe you would have to agree that in each issue there is something for everyone. Perhaps you enjoy the vintage article by Napoleon Hill or W. Clement Stone hand-picked from the archives, or the guest column that is written by a reader just like yourself, or my weekly column–certainly whatever part you read furthers your education regarding motivational self-help literature.

Week after week during regular work hours, vacations, and even seminars from home or away we have not missed a single issue, and it does not cost you a cent to subscribe. Considering this, I would like to ask a personal favor of you. In order to expand our readership, I am personally requesting that you have just one more person subscribe to our ezine–**one single person**. This can be accomplished by visiting our homepage at www.naphill.org and scrolling down to the bottom of the page. Once there you will see a photo of Napoleon Hill. It looks like this:

Your weekly inspirational ezine!

Have the person you sponsor enroll, or do it for them. Either way, it will increase our database by one person. And, every little bit helps, so make your contribution today by subscribing a friend, a relative, a co-worker, or an employee. Best of all, this little gift of service doesn't cost you a cent. But, when considering your personal success quotient we both know that it's what you DO that counts. **Thought + Action = Success**.

Help us help you. By enlisting a new subscriber our sphere of influence grows because of YOU! When you do something nice for someone else, it enhances your personal appearance. It gives you greater confidence in yourself and a psychological lift. Just by going the extra mile today, you do something for three people–me, the person you sponsor, and you too.

Thank you in advance for doing this kindness. You are appreciated. Hopefully, our numbers will indicate that success oriented people are doers! In W. Clement Stone's famous words: "Do it now!"

Seed of Thought

How to Win Friends and Influence People
by Dale Carnegie

Magic Seed 39

The most outstanding quality of leadership is willingness to make decisions. The person who won't or can't make decisions—after he has sufficient facts on which to base them—can never supervise others.

—NAPOLEON HILL

Dear Readers:

One required quality of any leader is decisiveness. Making decisions big and small is absolutely essential when serving as a leader. Decisions need to be made on a daily, monthly, and yearly basis, and when they are delayed the work flow becomes bottlenecked. You can learn to make quality decisions by forcing yourself to make some. People erroneously believe that if they postpone making decisions, they are incubating better ones. This is just another excuse in the long line of excuse making when it comes to decision making. Think about it. If you decide not to decide, you have made a decision! This indecision may buy you a little time, but it also gives you a delayed start.

Small decisions should be made quickly. Larger decisions made only after gathering all the pertinent facts. Each decision needs to be addressed on its own merit. Decisions as to what to eat for lunch, what to wear to the next social you attend, and what color is best suited for your new drapes are all important but do not require much time to make. However, decisions about your definite major purpose, your mastermind alliance, and your values and beliefs affect you for a lifetime and need to be given careful consideration.

By focusing on your long-term objectives when making daily decisions, you are building the foundation for your lifestyle brick by brick, or decision by decision. In considering a career, it is imperative that you make decisions that align with your career of choice. You cannot have a criminal record and remain a respected leader. You cannot abuse substances without career repercussions. You cannot be lazy and expect to make great strides. It all takes self-discipline, a positive mental attitude, controlled attention and effort, as well as a plan in place. By making good decisions you build a good life.

It has been said that where we are today in life is just a reflection of all the decisions that we have made along the way. Each decision points us in one direction or another. If we make decisions by whatever way the wind blows, we will never arrive in port. But, if we persistently make decisions in the direction of our true north, we will arrive at our destination on schedule or maybe even ahead of time.

Commit to being a decisive decision-maker. Make decisions that lead to your ultimate goal. Do not permit procrastination to undermine your effectiveness. Set your course to your ultimate purpose, and let the decisions you make bring you to your destiny one decisive decision at a time.

Seed of Thought

Acres of Diamonds
by R. H. Conwell

Magic Seed 40

Remember that true showmanship must follow a positive course. It never "knocks down" or minimizes the value of other people. No one can climb to success on someone else's shoulder.

–NAPOLEON HILL

Dear Readers:

The colors of fall are at their peak. Oranges, reds, yellows and greens jump at us from the trees as shafts of sunlight illuminate the sky's canvas. At just such times the magnificence can cause us to pause and marvel at literally how great the Universe is! This time of year the spotlight is truly on nature. Just being outdoors renews our enthusiasm and refreshes our entire being. Nature is a special elixir for those who revel in the beauty, spontaneity, and showmanship of Infinite Intelligence. This display of nature's perfection is preparing the canvas for our yearly fall celebration in Wise County, Virginia.

As I write this column, I am preparing to leave for Wise County, Virginia with friends and family to attend *Napoleon Hill Day* sponsored by Don Green, Executive Director of the Napoleon Hill Foundation, and his executive assistant Annedia Sturgill. Don Green together with Annedia's help does a remarkable job in recruiting the keynote speaker for over 700 high school students who come together Monday morning at the University of Virginia, College at Wise for their annual *Future Business Leaders of America* meeting that is so large it has to be held in the University's gymnasium. In the afternoon, the keynote speaker again addresses a smaller "hand-picked" audience that includes Board Trustees, relatives of Napoleon Hill, International Guests, the Napoleon Hill Scholars under the direction of Dr. Frey, invited guests, and local media covering the event. Putting this together yearly is no small task, but each year it gets better and better as Napoleon Hill is acknowledged for his writings that have impacted not only the local community, but the world at large. Hill's classic, ***Think and Grow Rich*** has been published in countless countries and has circled the globe numerous times. Each of us is the beneficiary of his research as long as we read the book and apply his teachings.

Don Green is the primary ambassador of Dr. Hill's works, and as always, he does a fantastic job of keeping the message front and center in the eyes of the world. Don's sense of mission is surpassed by none and his ability to keep Dr. Hill's materials front and center in the marketplace of motivational literature demonstrates not only his business acumen but his strong and lasting sense of dedication to the mission of the Napoleon Hill Foundation.

The 2008 keynote speaker for *Napoleon Hill Day* is Jim Connelly. He knows a little about showmanship too since he was the general manger of the Beverly Wilshire Hotel for a number of years. His friendships and associations include many of the "greats" worldwide, but he pledges his allegiance to Dr. Hill for not only helping him get his foot in the door when he was struggling to find employment, but enabling him to keep it there and climb the ladder to success. Jim is a strong personality with Irish charm who doesn't forget his roots and is not afraid to talk about them. We are privileged to have him address both audiences in Wise, Virginia.

Showmanship, as Dr. Hill states. . . "is creative. It has, as the name implies, a certain entertainment value. It demands ingenuity and a nice sense of timing." Both Don Green and Jim Connelly have mastered this and other aspects of what Napoleon Hill says it takes to be a leader. It is my distinct pleasure to work so closely with both of these practitioners of Dr. Hill's philosophy on a day-to-day basis.

Seed of Thought

A Lifetime of Riches
by Michael J. Ritt, Jr. & Kirk Landers

Magic Seed 41

Instead of worrying about the bad things that might befall you, spend a few minutes every day enumerating the pleasant events that will happen tomorrow, next week, next month, next year! By thinking about them, you will find yourself laying plans to make them happen! Then you are getting the habit of optimism.

–NAPOLEON HILL

Dear Readers:

Right now–I mean right now–grab a pen and paper and as quickly as you can make a list of 20 things that you are grateful for in your life this very minute. Don't stop and weigh each item, just do this spontaneously without a great deal of thought.

If you did as I asked, you forced your mind to make a conscious shift from neutrality or maybe even pessimism to optimism. Optimism is holding a positive outlook on life consciously. It is deciding for yourself that you will focus on the positive things life brings to you and thereby discount the negative. This is a decision that you make to improve not only your outlook on life, but your outcome too. Think about it. Positive cheerful thoughts condition our actions to bring about positive results. Thinking optimistically builds a mental pathway in our brain that disposes us to positive results.

There are many advantages to cultivating optimism. Here are a few:

- It lightens our load.
- It rejuvenates our spirit.
- It decreases wrinkles caused by worry.
- It alleviates the stress that brings headaches and other ailments.

- It improves our facial expressions.
- It calms us and paves the way for creativity and imagination to enter into our conscious thinking.
- It improves our situation because when creativity enters into our thinking, adversity and defeat are sent packing. The seed of equal or greater benefit is cultivated.
- It becomes a prayer of thanksgiving that is immediately heard by Infinite Intelligence. This activates the law of attraction and starts the "good news" process.
- It promotes generosity.
- It positively engages others.
- It assists us in being our best.
- It causes our hopes to soar.

All these things and more come from being optimistic. Let it be said that optimism opens doors that pessimism has nailed shut. Why would you choose to be anything else than optimistic? Try it for a few days cost free. It will be the best investment in yourself you ever made.

Seed of Thought

The Greatest Salesman in the World
by Og Mandino

Magic Seed 42

The person who is listless and lazy, lacking the spirit of adventure, is not the one who will achieve great things. Almost all men and women who attain high places in our civilization are "trouble-makers"—free spirits who aren't afraid to defy convention to strike out on new trails, to jar their fellowmen out of their lethargy.

—NAPOLEON HILL

Dear Readers:

It is not an easy job being a parent as any parent will tell you. Like being a teacher, before one tries out the profession most think that they can do the job with perfection since they were taught before too. Being children and students unfortunately is not the same as being capable parents and teachers. Dr. Hill recognizes this as he credits his step-mother with being a superb model on both accounts. She understood psychology and was determined to utilize it for the good of the family as she undertook the transformation of not only young Oliver Napoleon Hill, but also his father. To her credit, she orchestrated great advancements while capitalizing on her husband's and her step-son's positive traits thereby intentionally reducing their negative ones. She believed in the saying, "You get what you focus on." It was her decision to focus on improvement in her new family. Her efforts are detailed in the biography ***Lifetime of Riches*** that is available through the Napoleon Hill Foundation.

As we decide on our life's purpose, we can do the same. Challenges, obstacles, roadblocks, and various duties stand in our way oftentimes preventing us from becoming the person we know we can become. By underscoring the end result that we want through daily affirmation and positive mind conditioning we can get ourselves on track to the destination of our dreams. Numerous distractions can block our advancement, that is, until we recognize that focus followed by action determines our direction and ultimately our outcome in life. Why not hitch your wagon to a star, dream the impossible dream, stay the course, and win one for you this time? If not now, when? All we have is this day forward. Shouldn't we begin right now by making this day count for our life's purpose? You can achieve it if you believe it. Believe in yourself and the difference in your life will be all that you can imagine it will be.

Seed of Thought

The Alchemist
by Paulo Coelho & Alan R. Clarke

Magic Seed 43

The strongest trees of the forests aren't those most protected but those that must struggle against other trees—and surmount them—for survival.

—NAPOLEON HILL

Dear Readers:

Everyone has probably heard the expression: "That which does not kill you makes you stronger." It is a simple statement filled with truth. Overcoming adversities may just be the designated path that each of us is required to follow in order to grow into who we are meant to be. Problem is for some the purpose of the journey does not seem to be embraced and although the activity is completed, the lesson remains unlearned. That's why the saying, "If you do what you've always done, you'll get what you always got" is applicable in many lives—even our own.

How do we break out of this pattern of habit that ties us to unwanted results? If we can open ourselves to at least testing someone else's point of view, the trial might just prove to be worth it. Remember back when you were fearful of making a change because you knew what you liked and didn't want to experiment with anything different? This can happen when choosing food, clothes, friends, automobiles, restaurants, and anything else in which we have established a comfort zone, a pattern of behavior, a rut. Why not just explore a change in one small area today? Decide to be open versus closed. Seek out new horizons, tell yourself that it's okay to try this thing just for today because if it turns out not to your liking, you can always go back to the tried and true. Make risk-taking a game, and challenge yourself to play to win each and every time you decide to do something out of the ordinary—even extraordinary.

When I was young and complaining of boredom, my mother would tell me to get moving and do something—anything. It did not really matter what I did. Slowly but surely the cloud would lift and I would become re-invigorated by doing the task at hand. This works for depression too. It goes hand in hand with the "change your thoughts change your life" philosophy. By doing we become who we foresee ourselves becoming. Is it any wonder that when we struggle through adversities and arrive at the other side of the task that we are stronger and better prepared to meet the next hurdle? And, better yet when we learn a lesson such as the one of forgiveness that is contained in the book ***Radical Gratitude***, we are one step closer to being the person we were always meant to be.

Seed of Thought

I Can! The Key to Life's Golden Secrets
by Ben Sweetland

Magic Seed 44

One of the greatest of all truths lies in this fact:
When you are in difficulty and seemingly insurmountable problems are crowding you, look around until you find someone with an equal or greater problem than your own and try to help solve his problem. By the time you have helped the other fellow solve his problem, you will have miraculously found the solution to your own.

–NAPOLEON HILL

Dear Readers:

Going the Extra Mile is one of my favorite principles because it is so easy to use. Andrew Carnegie attributed his phenomenal success to this one principle and stated that he directly practiced it himself and indirectly through the people he hired. From an early age, this GEM of a principle can be instilled in the hearts of children and carried over into adulthood by parents who teach and nurture their children to consider others first. This practice pays big rewards as children mature and learn to be "go-givers" instead of "go-getters." There is something special about individuals who make you feel as if you are the most important person on the planet and that they are here to serve you! An attitude of service combined with an attitude of gratitude is a combination that cannot be beaten because it is so unusual and exceptional.

Still, many people misunderstand the workings of the Going the Extra Mile principle that Dr. Hill holds so dear. Oftentimes, people are heard to complain that when they have extended themselves for others that they are not the recipient of anything from the person they helped. They give to get, and when they don't receive they feel as if they have exerted undue effort in the wrong direction. This is a case of misunderstanding. Dr. Hill states that this principle involves doing more than you are paid to do without the expectation of anything additional in return. The average person then questions the rationale of doing the thing that Dr. Hill suggests. The "*What's In It For Me*?" question begins to rear its ugly head.

In a beautiful explanation as to why people give, Kahlil Gibran writes in ***The Prophet***:

> ***You often say, "I would give only to the deserving." The trees in your orchard say not so, nor the flocks on your pasture. They give that they may live, for to withhold is to perish.***

Of giving, Gibran also writes:

> ***There are those who give little of the much which they have–and they give it for recognition –and their hidden desire makes their gifts unwholesome.***
>
> ***And there are those who have little and give it all. These are the believers in life and the bounty of life, and their coffer is never empty.***
>
> ***There are those who give with joy, and that joy is their reward.***
>
> ***And there are those who give with pain, and that pain is their baptism.***
>
> ***And there are those who give and know not pain in giving, nor do they seek joy, nor give with mindfulness of virtue;***
>
> ***They give as in yonder valley the myrtle breathes its fragrance into space.***

I have to believe that Dr. Hill had these very ideas in mind when he wrote about the value of giving. It is easy to be a giver, but it is hard to cultivate the right motive for giving. If we remember the gift of the myrtle or even a

Christmas pine tree that freely gives its fragrance for all to enjoy, then we come to know the best manner of giving and the real purpose of gifting the gifts one has been given.

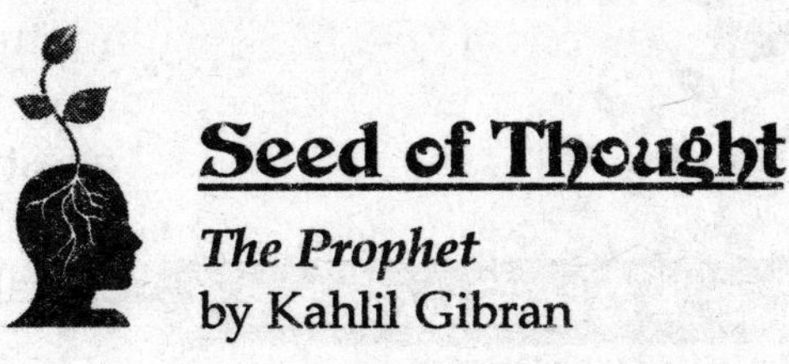

MORE SEEDS FOR SUCCESS

by Napoleon Hill

The mind grows through use; it atrophies through idleness.

Magic Seed 45

Failure often opens new doors to opportunity, and provides one with useful knowledge of the realities of life by the trial-and-error method. It also frequently reveals methods and plans which will not work, and cures vain people of their conceit.

–NAPOLEON HILL

Dear Readers:

This Thursday another Thanksgiving Day was celebrated in the United States and prayers of gratitude were heard around dinner tables nationwide. People are grateful for a variety of things, but usually not their failures. Seldom do we hear people expressing an attitude of gratitude for things that did not work out their way, for opportunities missed, for jobs lost, or for dreams unfulfilled. However, when lives are viewed in retrospect sometimes that lost opportunity opened up another door that led to an even greater gift. It seems hard to imagine, but historically this is proven correct time and time again.

When we reflect on the why and wherefore something happens that at the moment is not to our liking, we are focusing on the here and now and not the big picture. If we believe that we are put here on earth for a reason sometimes we must suspend our disbelief in what we envision to be the best outcome. It's been said that God always answers our prayers. Being skeptical, one person may complain that his prayer wasn't answered. God, being above reproach, responds, "Yes, I did answer your prayer. I said no." This little reminder of us not always being in control causes us to pause a moment and reconsider how our prayers might be heard.

Napoleon Hill frequently states that prayers of gratitude are the best possible type and that prayers of petition never work. It goes back to focusing on what is good and already positive in our lives, versus what is lacking. Begging, pleading, cajoling, bargaining, and generally whining are not things that bring about more good in our lives. Generosity, gratefulness, maintaining a positive mental attitude, enthusiasm, giving, going the extra mile, and putting others first bring about abundance in our lives.

This brief Gratitude Prayer authored by Dr. Hill, sums it up and is a good one to repeat daily as we prepare for the Holiday Season. It is not about getting but about giving, it is not about what I want, but what I can contribute, it is a message of abundance, and when spoken, will bring an overflow of goodness to you and yours. And, it is a reminder that we should be grateful for all the gifts we are given whether or not we are ready to receive them.

> I give thanks daily, not for mere riches, but for wisdom with which to recognize, embrace, and properly use the great abundance of riches I now have at my command. I have no enemies because I injure no man for any cause, but I try to benefit all with whom I come in contact, by teaching them the way to enduring riches. I have more material wealth than I need because I am free from greed and covet only the material things I can use while I live.

Seed of Thought

Try Giving Yourself Away

by David Dunn

Magic Seed 46

Anyone can wish for something–and most people do. But only a few know that a definite plan, backed with a burning desire, is the only means to achievement.

–NAPOLEON HILL

Dear Readers:

By reaching for the stars, we make a very positive statement to the Universe that we want the very best life has to offer. The simple act of reaching up is symbolic of aspiring toward higher goals and accomplishments. When we make a habit of looking up, we condition ourselves for future success because we program our mind for a positive outcome.

At this time of year in Indiana, the night skies can be crystal clear. When you arrive home after sunset, step out of your car, and look up on a clear night the spectacle of stars can be truly magical. With clarity you can see the Big Dipper, the North Star, and other signposts that astronomers love to point out. But, without even knowing the names of the constellations, the magnificence of the starscape is astounding. The air can be cold and crisp, yet simply by looking up one pauses to consider the glory of it all. This demonstration of Cosmic Habitforce in action brings to mind Dr. Hill's saying that "Cosmic Habitforce is the Comptroller of the Universe."

When we acknowledge the greatness of the Universe and the wonder of Infinite Intelligence at work, we can almost forget ourselves. And, I have been told that is exactly what we are supposed to do–remove ourselves–or at least distance ourselves–from the outcome. It's as if the timeless message of the Universe continually reminds us that all is right with the world–we do not have to be in control now or ever–someone else has our back.

In testimony to the above, consider the pure synchronicity of the meeting of Dr. Hill and W. Clement Stone in 1952. Neither of the two men planned the encounter, but once they met their lives and the lives of those they influenced changed forever. Like two thoroughbreds racing to the finish line, Stone accepted his dentist's invitation to attend a seminar/luncheon and Dr. Hill accepted the position of keynote speaker. The workings of the Universe served as a catalyst in bringing them together effortlessly. Before either one knew what was happening, they had committed to work with the other for a period of five years that grew into a decade. How remarkable is that? And, to think that it all happened so simplistically because both Dr. Hill and W. Clement Stone responded "yes" when they were asked to show up.

As you reach for the stars, don't forget to look up and throw your hat into the air as graduates do upon commencement. This is a signal to the Universe that you are open and ready to receive. Who knows what ultimate goodness awaits you!

Seed of Thought

PMA Science of Success Course
by Napoleon Hill

Magic Seed 47

Fear can be both a blessing and a curse, depending upon how and when one yields to it or rejects it.

–NAPOLEON HILL

Dear Readers:

Why be fearful when you can be faithful? Consider the two emotions as opposite sides of the same coin–"tails" represents fear and "heads" represents faith. By engaging in a coin toss, you expect a 50/50 outcome over time statistically. In life, however, we can create better odds than that by focusing on faith and intentionally weighing the odds in our favor. Logically, if we get what we focus on it makes better sense to focus on applied faith in its positive aspects rather than focusing on fear and its negative counterparts such as worry, depression, hatred, and almost everything that deals with lack.

The holiday season is characterized by giving and gratitude. It does not focus on lack and neglect. Yearly I enjoy attending a performance of *A Christmas Carol* by Charles Dickens because it always puts the reason for the season into perspective. I find it remarkable that when Scrooge–the grumpy, miserly, skinflint–has his transformation his new and improved self takes on each of the 17 Success Principles. For example, his **purpose becomes definite**–mankind becomes his "business," he **masterminds** with the local villagers and philanthropists to accomplish his ends in giving, his **applied faith** is reawakened when he realizes it is Christmas morning and he hasn't missed it, he **goes the extra mile** by astounding Tiny Tim's family with his generosity and caring, he exhibits a

pleasing personality by awakening his neighbors with his Christmas cheer, he displays **personal initiative, positive mental attitude, enthusiasm and self discipline** as he glimpses what life still has to offer him in the years ahead, he exercises **accurate thinking, controlled attention and teamwork** as he works with Bob, Tiny Tim's father, in planning a treatment plan for Tiny Tim, he learns his lesson in **adversity and defeat** as he is visited by the ghosts of Christmas Past, Present, and Yet to Come, he exercises **creative vision** in awakening the shopkeepers on Christmas morning to buy the holiday turkey and toys that will bring joy to the families, he decides to fully live his life and **maintain his sound health** and use rather than hoard his wealth through **budgeting his time and money**, and finally he credits **Cosmic Habitforce**—Infinite Intelligence—for sending him his wake-up call just in time for him to enjoy his life and live the remainder of it to the fullest. If Charles Dickens hadn't authored this book before Dr. Hill's classical works appeared, I would be convinced that he read it.

Spend an hour or two reading ***A Christmas Carol*** as a holiday gift to yourself. Then mentally review the 17 Success Principles and ask yourself whether they are fear-based or faith-based principles. I predict that you will find each one is a faith-based principle that helps us walk the path of life joyfully and with the expectation of receiving all the good that Infinite Intelligence has in mind for us. Give yourself the gift of faith this Holiday Season, and soon you will find that you are also adding the 17 Principles of Success to your own Christmas Stocking!

Seed of Thought

Paloma
Rich Winograd

Magic Seed 48

There is no substitute for this gift which only you can present to yourself. Its name is A POSITIVE MENTAL ATTITUDE. It costs nothing except the will to appropriate it; however, the only way you can keep it is to give it first position through usage in the habits which control your daily living.

–NAPOLEON HILL

Dear Readers:

During this holiday season many people reflect on the "perfect gift." Stores are turned topsy-turvy as shoppers compete to uncover that special present. "Seek and ye shall find" is taken literally and like prospectors looking for gold, shoppers persist in their mission.

Gifts given and gifts received are accompanied by special emotions at the time, but generally the spirit accompanying the gift may linger for awhile but not last a lifetime. Gifts that last a lifetime are extremely special and generally the hardest to locate.

In considering what would make an ideal gift, Dr. Hill suggests one that is economical, useful, attractive, and pleasing. He lists the benefits and suggests that there is even a good return on your investment. In fact, he proposes that you give this gift to yourself. As you use this gift, he promises that you will be the beneficiary of many good things to come. It appears that this is truly a gift that keeps on giving.

When you model this gift, people will notice and want the same thing for themselves. It promotes lightness in your step, a smile in your voice, a song in your heart, a twinkle in your eye, an attitude of gratitude in your heart, and an appreciation in your spirit for all you have been given in your life.

Dr. Hill's ultimate gift is the gift of a Positive Mental Attitude. You may have guessed that already. Why not decide to gift it to yourself this holiday season? You will be the better for it. And, by the way, so will everyone else who comes into contact with you. Spread the good news and make this gift to yourself one that lasts a lifetime.

Seed of Thought

Napoleon Hill's Golden Rules
by Napoleon Hill

Magic Seed 49

Pointing my finger at the man in the mirror I said, "There is the man who can help you. He is the only man who can do it, and until you become better acquainted with him and learn to depend upon him you will not find your way out of your present unfortunate condition."

—NAPOLEON HILL

Dear Readers:

When we look in the mirror many times daily do we see ourselves or simply the reflection of outward appearances? What does it mean to really look at yourself and know that you are connecting with your true essence, the eternal you that is capable of living a life of abundance and beauty?

Normally speaking, too much self-awareness can be hard to process when we rise in the morning and catch a glimpse of our passing selves. At noon too we might straighten our hair and give ourselves a once over glance, but too quickly to connect with our unique spirit. Finally, at night when we brush our teeth and prepare for sleep, we probably don't even concern ourselves with looking picture perfect. Day in, day out we repeat these actions and never really take the time to catch a glimpse of our true nature—that eternal self which is timeless and ageless. Maybe it is time that we face the man or woman in the mirror and look deeper than simply outward appearances.

Dr. Hill has the prescription for an ailing spirit and waning self-esteem. He pulls back the office curtain in his famous story, and directs the tramp to really look at the only person who is capable of making a positive change in his life–himself! The eternal truth is that the only person who can change us is ourselves. Sometimes this message is not easily received because it is too easy for people to rely on others to fix what is broken in their lives. Problems are too often given to parents, spouses, teachers, employers, agencies, organizations, governments, friends, co-workers, pastors–you name it–to fix for us, when the very answer we seek lies dormant in ourselves. Until we accept the fact that both the problem and the cure are within us, no critical change can or will occur.

In Dr. Hill's story, the tramp leaves in a rush after facing the mirror and it is assumed that he is insulted. Months later, however, the man returns and thanks Dr. Hill for making him see reality. By really looking in the mirror at himself, he determined that it was he who was causing the problem and that only he was the one who could fix it. This is applied psychology at its best.

Give yourself several minutes to really look into your eyes today–the windows to your soul–as we approach the New Year. Ask yourself what the person in the mirror has to do with who you are and how you live your life. If a change is in order, begin right now, today to make the change that will place you on the road to success that is already there inside of you. You are the treasure, the ultimate gift, the perfect outcome, the buried gold, and the shining star. All this is there for you to see as you look in the mirror!

Seed of Thought

How to Sell Your Way Through Life
by Napoleon Hill

Magic Seed 50

Generally speaking there are two types of minds–the type which has been conditioned to believe in success, to demand it, and usually finds it; and the type which, by neglect in the formation of a success consciousness, has been conditioned to expect poverty and failure, and usually finds these.

–NAPOLEON HILL

Dear Readers:

What habits do you want to cultivate? This is not a simple question to be glossed over lightly because whatever habits we create in our lives determine our destiny. Habits may be likened to character building blocks. One by one they are cemented together to form a strong fortress that serves to repel good or evil. Walls serve to keep things out or to keep things in. Our habits over time become our character, therefore selecting good habits predisposes us to a strong character that will serve us well now and in the future.

By voluntarily selecting good habits, we are conditioning ourselves in advance for positive outcomes. To be effective, habits must become habitual or rote meaning that we do them spontaneously without giving them much thought. Like tying our shoes, doing the dishes, driving the car, combing our hair, or just about anything that we do on autopilot was once a learned practice that became routine due to repetition.

Much like a computer program, our habits enable us to perform many daily tasks without conscious thought. We program ourselves for success or failure early in life by the thoughts and activities that we choose to incorporate into our daily thinking. Once our character begins to take shape our destiny follows as well. What good we do or what evil we do can be traced back to early habitual thoughts, desires, and or emotions that eventually were manifested in the physical world in the form of actions taken based on motives related to thoughts coupled with our feelings.

In the New Year, many of us wish to address changes that we like to call resolutions, but they would be better enacted as habits. Resolutions aid in pointing us in the right direction, but positive habits move us forward one action at a time.

Consider things that could be improved in your life that involve current actions you now take. Perhaps you sleep too late, watch too much television, fail to exercise, let the supper dishes sit in the sink until morning, eat wrong food choices, procrastinate when it comes to paperwork, etc., these are all potential targets for changes in habits. Begin simply with one or two choices at a time, and monitor your progress. Before a change can become a habit, it takes many repetitions to make it become part of your programming. Give yourself time. Make positive changes. You can teach an old dog new tricks–and even cats too–it just may take a little more time, effort and determination. But, after all, we're worth it because we are the best we have to work with! By this time next year, you could be a new you with an expanded support system of good habits to propel you further toward your life's purpose. As W. Clement Stone was fond of saying, "Do it now!" There is no better time.

Seed of Thought

The Richest Man in Babylon
by George S. Clason

Magic Seed 51

All of us are endowed with an intuition, a sort of sixth sense resulting from our experience, by which we seem automatically to know whether a person is telling truth or falsehood.

–NAPOLEON HILL

Dear Readers:

Being sincere with ourselves first helps us to be sincere with others later. Sincerity means speaking truthfully in a direct manner. Not beating around the bush, not cushioning our remarks to make them more palatable, not considering what's in it for me, but delivering our message in a straightforward manner in order to promote understanding. This understanding based on direct talk is intended to move everyone forward concerning whatever current concern there is.

Sincere people do not place blame, criticize, find fault, or gossip. Their interest lies in examining the issues at hand in an open conversation, resolving any confusion that may exist, and then anticipating and mutually working towards the best results possible. Likewise, when we are sincere with ourselves, we do not attempt to cover up our real motives, but rather look deeply within our spiritual presence in order to understand ourselves better.

Sincere people are sought after for advice and counsel. People tend to respect a sincere person because they know that they will receive a straight response without the extra verbiage. In sincerity less is more and people recognize messages with meaning that speak from the heart.

As you speak today, why not focus on being direct and sincere in your statements? This does not imply that you are abrupt or inconsiderate, but rather that you are focusing first on getting the right message across. Mean what you say and say what you mean. This method might just become a good habit to cultivate in the year ahead.

Sincerity offers opportunities to adjust and correct misunderstandings. Through sincerity we learn more about another's point of view, and whether we agree or not it still gives us the opportunity to engage in a dialog that can lead to greater understanding and eventually peace. Personal peace, peace in the home, peace in communities, peace in the nation and peace in the world is a progressive movement that can begin with each individual who practices sincerity. Why not begin today by practicing sincerity. It will make the world a better place.

Seed of Thought

Secret of the Ages
by Robert Collier

Magic Seed 52

The most intense yearning of every normal person is for recognition of his value and worth as an individual human being.

—NAPOLEON HILL

Dear Readers:

Psychologists report that every person's basic, primary desire is to be recognized and affirmed for the positive contributions they make in life. This motive is said to surpass all others. It makes good sense when you think about it because our deeds are the only thing that we are able to take with us as we transition from this life to the next.

On January 1, 2009, the Napoleon Hill World Learning Center lost a good friend and strong supporter, Michael (Mike) Frain. Mike lost his courageous battle with cancer, but he never lost his positive mental attitude. Throughout his illness, Mike assured us that he would beat this disease. He remained upbeat and strong as he struggled. When he visited us, he supported us more than we supported him. His presence gave us renewed hope in the meaning of life. Sometimes he just stopped in to visit, sometimes he cooked lunch and served it, and other times he stayed longer and participated in our workshops. And, sometimes, magically in a meditation that he created, he could even make it "rain." Whenever he was here, we were uplifted by his presence.

I remember Mike most as a counselor. He was not so much a giver of advice as he was a strong listener who tried to discern how a person needed to be heard at that moment. Several times he showed up at my door and simply asked, "What's wrong?" He then would indicate that he felt an intuitive pull to come and see me. Usually his introduction was followed by a session where I mainly talked and he listened. And, afterwards I always felt the better for it.

Mike could remind a person of an Irish imp or even a leprechaun if one looked closely. He did have the gift of blarney and liked often to reference his Irish heritage. His eyes twinkled and his smile was contagious. He always left a person with a firm handshake, a pat on the back, a kind word on his lips, and a promise to return soon. He emailed often to stay in touch when he could not visit in person, and he always wished the very best for everyone. Mike was a person who always had you covered or in today's terminology he had your back. His uncanny ability to show up when needed still astounds me, and I expect him to be around now more than before.

In remembering Mike, Chino Martinez, executive assistant at the Napoleon Hill World Learning Center, remarked that Mike always appreciated great philosophers and loved the quote by Goethe that states: "Whatever you can do, or dream you can, begin it. Boldness has genius, power, and magic in it." Chino notes that Mike always shared his boldness, genius, power and magic with everyone he met.

And, Mike, if truth be told, your magic did create a lot of ripples in people's ponds. You made a difference and I for one am glad that you were sent to be our "greeter" when the Center opened at Purdue University Calumet in 2000. I know that you changed many lives by being who you are and many eyes--Irish and otherwise--smile because of you.

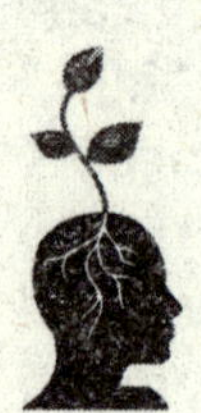

Seed of Thought

The Purpose Driven Life
by Rick Warren

APPENDIX

Quotations:

Seed 1: *Your capacity to believe is your greatest potential asset.*

—NAPOLEON HILL

Seed 2: *Friendship rates with love as one of life's most precious assets. But like every desirable thing, friendship isn't free. There's a price on it which depends on the nature of the individual with whom you enjoy this coveted relationship.*

—NAPOLEON HILL

Seed 3: *When a person is struggling for recognition and advancement, seldom does he find anyone to give him a boost. But once he makes the grade, people stand in line to offer him help.*

—NAPOLEON HILL

Seed 4: *Whether ailing or not, I know of nothing that will bring peace of mind and sound health more quickly than the habit of counting one's blessings and recognizing them in a prayer of gratitude.*

—NAPOLEON HILL

Seed 5: *Every ship in a fleet must make contact with the flagship at regular stated hours, whether or not there is anything to report.*

—NAPOLEON HILL

Seed 6: *The successful person has learned that "whatever the mind of man can conceive and believe the mind of man can achieve." And this person keeps on keeping on until he converts his stumbling blocks into stepping stones. He knows that with every adversity comes the seed of an equivalent benefit.*

—NAPOLEON HILL

Seed 7: *If you can't do great things yourself, remember that you can do small things in a great way.*

—NAPOLEON HILL

Seed 8: *Analysis of men and women in the upper brackets of success, in a variety of callings, reveals the astounding fact that each individual attained success in almost exact proportion to the adversities and defeats which had been met with and overcome.*

–NAPOLEON HILL

Seed 9: *There is one human being on whom one can depend, without disappointment, in time of adversity, and this is one's self.*

–NAPOLEON HILL

Seed 10: *First, all achievements, all successes and all desires begin with a clear mental image of one's goal–a definite picture of what you desire from life. Unless you know where you want to go, how can you get there?*

–NAPOLEON HILL

Seed 11: *Success doesn't crown the person who sells himself short through lack of self-confidence. But it does favor the person who knows what he wants, is determined to get it, and frowns at the word impossible.*

–NAPOLEON HILL

Seed 12: *The subconscious has one very peculiar trait, it believes everything one tells it, and acts accordingly. It not only believes and acts upon one's spoken words, but more astounding still, it believes in and acts upon one's thoughts;* ***especially those thoughts which are highly emotionalized with either faith or fear.***

–NAPOLEON HILL

Seed 13: *You can be a man with a grievance or a man with a message; you can be a BUILDER or a DESTROYER, but make sure of this, that you can no more tear down without in turn being torn down, than you could sow wild mustard and reap a harvest of oats.*

–NAPOLEON HILL

Seed 14: *Plant the seed of service that is right in quality and quantity, then watch what happens when you have established the reputation of being a person who always renders better service than that which is paid for.*

–NAPOLEON HILL

Seed 15: *Single-handed no man can accomplish enough to cause much of a stir; but, through allied effort Rockefeller became the world's richest man, Henry Ford has astounded the world and put the most learned men to shame by comparison, James J. Hill got up from the telegraph key and became the greatest builder of railroads, and George Washington carved his name at the head of the list of immortal patriots.*

–NAPOLEON HILL

Seed 16: *I will not engage in any business or sport that implies fraud, cruelty or injustice to any living thing.*

–NAPOLEON HILL

Seed 17: *Education comes from within; you get it by struggle and effort and thought.*

–NAPOLEON HILL

Seed 18: *The Counsel Table around which I gather, with these great men of the past each night, is an imaginary one, but the messages which they left behind them are real, and I am using this method of burning them deeply into my consciousness, that their influence may find its way into the pattern after which my character is being built.*

–NAPOLEON HILL

Seed 19: *Time is the only priceless treasure in the universe!*

–NAPOLEON HILL

Seed 20: *In the mad rush for glory and fame and dollars let us not forget the hand that rocks the cradle. We may not raise ourselves in the estimate of men, by honoring her as she is entitled to be honored, but, by doing so we are not apt to lower ourselves in the eyes of God.*

–NAPOLEON HILL

Seed 21: *Wherever there is work to be done you can find a chance to become a leader. It may be humble leadership, at first, but the leadership becomes a habit and soon the most humble leader becomes a powerful man of action and he is then sought for greater leadership.*

–NAPOLEON HILL

Seed 22: *You have within you a sleeping giant who is ready to be awakened and directed by you to the performance of any sort of service you desire. And when you wake up some morning and find yourself on the success beam and in the upper brackets of success, you will wonder why you had not sooner discovered that you had all of the makings of a big success.*

–NAPOLEON HILL

Seed 23: *Sometimes it is wiser to join forces with an opponent than it is to fight.*

–NAPOLEON HILL

Seed 24 *Concentration is the ability, through fixed habit and practice, to keep your mind on one subject until you have thoroughly familiarized yourself with that subject and mastered it.*

–NAPOLEON HILL

Seed 25: *The richest copper mind in the world was discovered by a miner who had spent most of his life searching for gold. This trusty mule, which carried all of his worldly belongings, including his mining equipment, fell into a gopher hole, broke his leg and had to be shot. While trying to dig the mule's leg out of the hole, the rich copper ore was uncovered.*

–NAPOLEON HILL

Seed 26: *Remember that those things that have never been done before offer the greatest challenge and opportunity. The pioneer who first accomplishes them is the one who reaps the reward.*

–NAPOLEON HILL

Seed 27: *Patience demands its own peculiar kind of courage. It's a persistent type of forbearance and fortitude that results from complete dedication to an ideal or goal. Therefore, the more strongly you are imbued with the idea of achieving your principal goal in life, the more patience you will have to overcome obstacles.*

–NAPOLEON HILL

Seed 28: *I refuse to believe what you say unless it harmonizes with what you do.*

–NAPOLEON HILL

Seed 29: *The necessity for struggle is one of the unique ways that the Creator has provided to force people to develop and expand their mind-powers and gain wisdom. Wherever that necessity is removed the individual becomes soft and lacking in the resourcefulness with which to avail himself of his worldly needs.*

–NAPOLEON HILL

Seed 30: *Any person who attains a high degree of success usually starts off by putting everything they have behind a single objective. They stay on a single track until they get to their destination. After that, they may branch out by setting new goals for themselves.*

–NAPOLEON HILL

Seed 31: *A positive mental attitude brings with it faith, enthusiasm, personal initiative, self-discipline, imagination and definiteness of purpose which attract people and beneficial opportunities.*

–NAPOLEON HILL

Seed 32: *The successful person has a keen respect for his Creator and expresses it frequently through prayers and deeds of helpfulness to others. The failure believes in nothing but his own desire for food and shelter, and seeks these at the expense of others when and where he can.*

–NAPOLEON HILL

Seed 33: *Flexibility is the one trait that softens poverty and adorns riches for it helps you to be grateful for your blessings and unabashed by misfortune. It can help you, too, to make beneficial use of every experience of life, whether pleasant or unpleasant.*

–NAPOLEON HILL

Seed 34: *No one is "born enthusiastic." It is a trait that is acquired. You can acquire it, too. Remember that in almost every contact with others you are trying, in a sense, to sell them something. That's true in all except* *trivial relationships. First convince yourself of the value of your idea, your product, your service–or yourself. Examine it–or yourself–critically. Learn the flaws in whatever you are trying to sell–and eliminate or correct them. Be thoroughly convinced of the "rightness" of your product or idea.*

–NAPOLEON HILL

Seed 35: *Is it possible that you have imprisoned your mind in a social and cultural concentration camp? Have you subjected yourself to a brain-washing of your own making, isolating you from ideas that could lead to success? If so, it's time to sweep aside the bars of prejudice that imprison your intellect.*

–NAPOLEON HILL

Seed 36: *Without humility you will never be able to find what I call the "seed of equivalent benefit" in adversity and defeat. Every adversity or defeat, I have found, carries with it something to help you overcome it–and even rise above it.*

–NAPOLEON HILL

Seed 37: *Then learn to use the right word in the right place at the right time. This comes only from practice in everyday conversation. As of this moment, erase completely from your vocabulary all profanity, blasphemy, obscenity, or irreverence. The use of profanity or blasphemy is a dead giveaway that one lacks the word-power to express his emotions properly. Obscenity, off-color jokes and the double entendre are resorted to only by the boor who lacks the cleverness to be really funny or amusing. Irreverence, to one's own Deity or that of others, is always in unforgivably bad taste.*

–NAPOLEON HILL

Seed 38: *Rightly or wrongly, human nature is such that first impressions usually are the ones that endure. More important, the first impression may be the only one we have a chance to make. Therefore, it must be good!*

–NAPOLEON HILL

Seed 39: *The most outstanding quality of leadership is willingness to make decisions. The person who won't or can't make decisions–after he has sufficient facts on which to base them–can never supervise others.*

–NAPOLEON HILL

Seed 40: *Remember that true showmanship must follow a positive course. It never "knocks down" or minimizes the value of other people. No one can climb to success on someone else's shoulder.*

–NAPOLEON HILL

Seed 41: *Instead of worrying about the bad things that might befall you, spend a few minutes every day enumerating the pleasant events that will happen tomorrow, next week, next month, next year! By thinking about them, you will find yourself laying plans to make them happen! Then you are getting the habit of optimism.*

–NAPOLEON HILL

Seed 42: *The person who is listless and lazy, lacking the spirit of adventure, is not the one who will achieve great things. Almost all men and women who attain high places in our civilization are "trouble-makers"–free spirits who aren't afraid to defy convention to strike out on new trails, to jar their fellowmen out of their lethargy.*

–NAPOLEON HILL

Seed 43: *The strongest trees of the forests aren't those most protected but those that must struggle against other trees–and surmount them–for survival.*

–NAPOLEON HILL

Seed 44: One of the greatest of all truths lies in this fact: *When you are in difficulty and seemingly insurmountable problems are crowding you, look around until you find someone with an equal or greater problem than your own and try to help solve his problem. By the time you have helped the other fellow solve his problem, you will have miraculously found the solution to your own.*

–NAPOLEON HILL

Seed 45: *Failure often opens new doors to opportunity, and provides one with useful knowledge of the realities of life by the trial-and-error method. It also frequently reveals methods and plans which will not work, and cures vain people of their conceit.*

–NAPOLEON HILL

Seed 46: *Anyone can wish for something–and most people do. But only a few know that a definite plan, backed with a burning desire, is the only means to achievement.*

–NAPOLEON HILL

Seed 47: *Fear can be both a blessing and a curse, depending upon how and when one yields to it or rejects it.*

–NAPOLEON HILL

Seed 48: *There is no substitute for this gift which only you can present to yourself. Its name is* A POSITIVE MENTAL ATTITUDE. *It costs nothing except the will to appropriate it; however, the only way you can keep it is to give it first position through usage in the habits which control your daily living.*

–NAPOLEON HILL

Seed 49: *Pointing my finger at the man in the mirror I said, "There is the man who can help you. He is the* ***only man*** *who can do it, and until you become better acquainted with him and learn to depend upon him you will not find your way out of your present unfortunate condition."*

–NAPOLEON HILL

Seed 50: *Generally speaking there are two types of minds–the type which has been conditioned to believe in success, to demand it, and usually finds it; and the type which, by neglect in the formation of a success consciousness, has been conditioned to expect poverty and failure, and usually finds these.*

–NAPOLEON HILL

Seed 51: *All of us are endowed with an intuition, a sort of sixth sense resulting from our experience, by which we seem automatically to know whether a person is telling truth or falsehood.*

–NAPOLEON HILL

Seed 52: *The most intense yearning of every normal person is for recognition of his value and worth as an individual human being.*

—NAPOLEON HILL

Recommended Reading:

1. W. Clement Stone . . . *The Success System That Never Fails*
2. Napoleon Hill . . . . . . *You Can Work Your Own Miracles*
3. Viktor E. Frankl . . . . *Man's Search for Meaning*
4. Napoleon Hill . . . . . . *Grow Rich With Peace of Mind*
5. Napoleon Hill . . . . . . *Keys to Success: The 17 Principles of Personal Achievement*
6. J. Martin Kohe. . . . . . *Your Greatest Power*
7. W. Clement Stone . . . *Believe and Achieve*
8. Napoleon Hill . . . . . . *Think and Grow Rich*
9. W. Clement Stone and Napoleon Hill . . . *Success Through a Positive Mental Attitude*
10. Napoleon Hill and Michael J. Ritt . . . . . . *Keys to Positive Thinking*
11. George Matthew Adams . . . . *You Can*
12. Arnold Fox, M. D. and Barry Fox, Ph. D . . . *Making Miracles*
13. Napoleon Hill . . . . . . *The Wisdom of Andrew Carnegie*
14. J. Martin Kohe and Judith Williamson . . *How to Become a Mental Millionaire*
15. Og Mandino . . . . *A Treasury of Success Unlimited*
16. Napoleon Hill and Judith Williamson . . *Fifty-Two Lessons for Life*
17. Cavett Robert . . . . . . *Success with People*
18. Dr. Joseph Murphy . . *The Power of Your Subconscious Mind*

19. Arnold Fox, M.D. . . . *Wake Up! You're Alive*
and Barry Fox, Ph. D
20. Napoleon Hill and . . *Poems that Inspire You to Think*
Judith Williamson *and Grow Rich*
21. Napoleon Hill . . . . . . *Law of Success*
22. Andrew Bienkowski . *Radical Gratitude*
and Mary Akers
23. Ella Wheeler Wilcox . *Poems of Ella Wheeler Wilcox*
24. Napoleon Hill . . . . . . *Napoleon Hill's Positive Action Plan: 365 Meditations for Making Each Day a Success*
25. Claude Bristol . . . . . . *The Power of Believing*
26. Venice Bloodworth . . *Key to Yourself*
27. Napoleon Hill . . . . . . *Napoleon Hill's First Editions*
28. Charlie "T" Jones. . . . *Life is Tremendous*
29. Ralph Waldo Emerson . *Collected Works of Ralph Waldo Emerson*
30. Napoleon Hill . . . . . . *Think and Grow Rich Action Pack*
31. Norman Vincent Peale . *The Power of Positive Thinking*
32. Napoleon Hill . . . . . . *Succeed and Grow Rich Through Persuasion*
33. Arnold Fox, M.D. . . . *Beyond Positive Thinking*
and Barry Fox, Ph.D
34. Napoleon Hill . . . . . . *The Master-Key to Riches*
35. Viktor E. Frankl . . . . *Man's Search for Ultimate Meaning*
36. Napoleon Hill and . . *Timeless Thoughts for Today*
Judith Williamson
37. Florence Scovel Shinn . *Your Word Is Your Wand*
38. Dale Carnegie . . . . . . *How to Win Friends and Influence People*
39. R. H. Conwell . . . . . . *Acres of Diamonds*
40. Michael J. Ritt, Jr. . . . *A Lifetime of Riches*
and Kirk Landers
41. Og Mandino . . . . *The Greatest Salesman in the World*
42. Paulo Coelho and . . . *The Alchemist*
Alan R. Clarke

43. Ben Sweetland . . . . . *I Can! The Key to Life's Golden Secrets*
44. Kahlil Gibran. . . . . . . *The Prophet*
45. David Dunn. . . . . *Try Giving Yourself Away*
46. Napoleon Hill . . . . . . *PMA Science of Success Course*
47. Rich Winograd . . . . . *Paloma*
48. Napoleon Hill . . . . . . *Napoleon Hill's Golden Rules*
49. Napoleon Hill . . . . . . *How to Sell Your Way Through Life*
50. George S. Clason . . . *The Richest Man in Babylon*
51. Robert Collier . . . . . . *Secret of the Ages*
52. Rick Warren . . . . *The Purpose Driven Life*

For additional information about Napoleon Hill products please contact the following locations:

Napoleon Hill World Learning Center
Purdue University Calumet
2300 173rd Street
Hammond, IN 46323-2094

Judith Williamson, Director
Uriel "Chino" Martinez, Assistant/Graphic Designer

Telephone: 219-989-3173 or 219-989-3166
email: nhf@calumet.purdue.edu

Napoleon Hill Foundation
University of Virginia-Wise
College Relations Apt. C
1 College Avenue
Wise, VA 24293

Don Green, Executive Director
Annedia Sturgill, Executive Assistant

Telephone: 276-328-6700
email: napoleonhill@uvawise.edu

Website: www.naphill.org